EATING
— THE —
Pacific Northwest

REDISCOVERING REGIONAL
AMERICAN FLAVORS

DARRIN NORDAHL

Copyright © 2018 by Darrin Nordahl
First edition
Published by Chicago Review Press Incorporated
814 North Franklin Street
Chicago, Illinois 60610
ISBN 978-1-61373-528-2

Library of Congress Cataloging-in-Publication Data
Names: Nordahl, Darrin, author.
Title: Eating the Pacific Northwest / Darrin Nordahl.
Description: First edition. | Chicago, Illinois : Chicago Review Press
   Incorporated, [2018] | Series: Rediscovering regional American flavors |
   Includes bibliographical references and index.
Identifiers: LCCN 2018021676 (print) | LCCN 2018022881 (ebook) |
ISBN
   9781613735299 (Pdf) | ISBN 9781613735305 (Mobipocket) | ISBN
9781613735312
   (Epub) | ISBN 9781613735282 (cloth)
Subjects: LCSH: Cooking, American—Pacific Northwest style. | LCGFT:
   Cookbooks.
Classification: LCC TX715.2.P32 (ebook) | LCC TX715.2.P32 N66 2018
(print) |
   DDC 641.59795—dc23
LC record available at https://lccn.loc.gov/2018021676

Interior design: Sarah Olson
Layout: Jonathan Hahn
All photos by Darrin Nordahl, unless otherwise noted

Printed in the United States of America
5 4 3 2 1

For Kess

"Hey, sweet baby
Don't you think maybe
We can find us a brand-new recipe?"

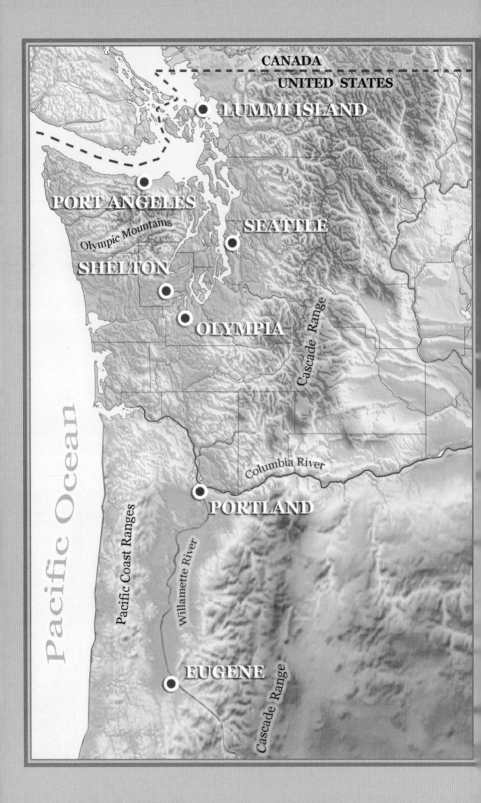

CONTENTS

PROLOGUE: IDENTITY CRISIS   1
INTRODUCTION: WHAT IS THE PACIFIC NORTHWEST?   11

1. EUGENE: BLISS FOOD   17
   Truffled Pecorino Cheese   41
   Buttermilk Fried Oysters with Truffled Rémoulade   43
   Black Truffle Pasta with Marsala Cream and Foie Gras   46
   Dungeness Crab and White Truffle Tartlets   49

2. SHELTON: FROM TIDE TO TABLE   53
   Oyster Martini   67
   Xinh's Geoduck Ceviche   70
   Geoduck Fritters with Rémoulade   73
   Geoduck Deep-Dish Pie   76

3. OLYMPIA: IT'S THE WATER   83

4. PORT ANGELES: LOBSTER OF THE PACIFIC   97
   Dungeness Crab Bisque   115
   Dungeness Crab Quiche   118
   Dungeness Crab Shooters   121
   Dungeness Crab Omelet   124

5. PORTLAND: BOUNTY IN THE BRAMBLE 127

Marionberry Cocktail 152

Marionberry, Salmon, and Prawn Lettuce Cups 154

Roasted Duck and Broccolini with Huckleberry Relish 156

Wild Oregon Berries with Limoncello Cream 159

6. SEATTLE: KING OF KINGS 161

*Pan Roasted Marbled Chinook with
    Sugar Snap Peas, Radish, and Morels* 175

Duna Chowder 178

Grilled Marbled Chinook and Summer Vegetables 181

7. LUMMI ISLAND: HYPERLOCAL 187

Pickled Wild Things 211

Nootka Roses and Salmonberries 213

Buckwheat Crepe and Huckleberry Compote 216

RESOURCES: WHEN YOU GO 219
INDEX 227

At its heart, a genuine food culture is an affinity between the people and the land that feeds them.

—Barbara Kingsolver, *Animal, Vegetable, Miracle*

My meals shake [folks] from their routines, not only of meat-potatoes-gravy, but of thought, of behavior.

—M. F. K. Fisher, *The Gastronomical Me*

* * *

INDIGENOUS: a species whose presence in a region is the result of only natural resources and means, without any human intervention. Synonymous with *native*.

prologue

IDENTITY CRISIS

Road sign on US-101 along the Oregon coast.

I recently came across a fascinating bit of archaeology theory, and it completely changed my notion of American food.

About eight thousand years ago, the part of North America we now call the continental United States was heavily peopled. Archaic Indians, as archaeologists refer to them, banded together in tribes from Puget Sound to the Gulf of California to Chesapeake Bay. Gone were the mastodons, mammoths, saber-toothed tigers, and other megafauna; they disappeared with the retreating glaciers at the end of the Ice Age. Elk, bison, deer, rabbits, and squirrels were now the dominant wildlife. The boreal forests also retreated, replaced with deciduous hardwoods. Fruits and nuts abounded. Sea levels rose as the massive polar ice sheet melted, filling bays and estuaries. Ducks, geese, fish, and crustaceans flourished. The climate was warmer and drier than at the end of the Ice Age, and grasses proliferated. The American landscape eight thousand years ago was strikingly similar to today's.

What struck me most was the Archaic Indian diet. Archaeologists believe those ancient Americans consumed some 120 different species of plants and animals. Now, I'm a foodie who takes pride in my diverse diet. Beef bores me. I prefer goat and lamb and elk. Chicken is bland, but duck and pigeon excite my palate. I'll take fava beans over green beans and persimmons over apples. I garnish my eggs with chervil and I season my fish with sumac. I know food and I eat it all. Still, 120 different plants and animals?

I began to doubt my own diet—was it as diverse as I thought it was? I grabbed a piece of paper and jotted down all the foods—plant, animal, and fungus—I routinely consume as part of my annual menu. After about half an hour, I felt I had a fairly representative list of my yearly ingredients: 132 items. *Aha! I have beaten you, prehistoric American settler!* But the desire to launch into celebratory chest-thumping and nasal grunting quickly passed; it was a hollow victory, to be sure. I looked back at my list of foods and realized something unsettling. *Bananas. Coffee. Mangoes.* I was clearly benefitting from our global system of agriculture. Thanks to foods from faraway lands, I can consume a respectable diversity of ingredients. I am part of a culture eight thousand years more evolved (supposedly) than that of ancient America, able to eat food from all over the world. The

Archaic Indians didn't have such convenience. Yet, my diet is hardly more diverse than that ancient society's, whose food shed consisted of little more than a few dozen square miles. They were the original locavores.

But if those early Americans weren't consuming bananas, coffee, and mangoes, what were they eating? Corn, beans, and squash—the Three Sisters of the Native American diet—was my immediate guess. But I was wrong. Those three foods are domesticated crops that originated in Mesoamerica. For the Archaic Indians, who were hunters and gatherers, agriculture would come thousands of years later. And they certainly didn't hunt cows, pigs, or chickens, since these creatures were just beginning to be domesticated in Eurasia at the time.

"What about avocados and artichokes?" I thought. They've always struck me as prehistoric-looking foods, the kind that might have grown here since the dinosaurs roamed. But at the time of the Archaic Indians, avocados hadn't yet left their home-land of south central Mexico and artichokes were still nestled around the Mediterranean. It turns out our Florida oranges originally came from China as did Georgia peaches. I know papaya and pineapple aren't American natives, but perhaps the apple is? Nope. The quintessential American fruit is a Colonial-era adoption, arriving in the States via a circuitous route from Kazakhstan. Carrots likely originated in Persia, potatoes in Peru, and onions in West Pakistan. You can guess where Brussels sprouts originated.

Nuts were certainly staples in the ancient American diet, but not almonds or pistachios (natives of the Middle East) or cashews or Brazil nuts (natives of Brazil). Peanuts—if you want to think of them as nuts—hail from Peru. The prehistoric settlers did eat walnuts—just not the ones we Americans today commonly eat, the so-called English walnut, which is a native of Kyrgyzstan.

As I continued to research the foods of the Archaic Indians, I could piece together a modest list of American ingredients that were tasty enough and readily accessible in their immediate surrounds, though I was nowhere near their 120-item grocery list. That they consumed ten dozen indigenous plants and animals astonished me. But this wasn't nearly as astonishing as *my* 132 items. Save for cranberries, turkey, blueberries, blackberries, salmon, pecans, and sunflower seeds, my diverse diet was only possible because some ten dozen foods I typically consume come from everywhere *but* the United States. When I looked over my list and in my pantry and refrigerator, I realized the great irony of American food: American ingredients—true American produce—are scarcely present in American cuisine.

Some argue this is precisely what makes American cuisine American. Like the founding families of our nation, our produce is a soup-pot of immigrants hailing from every corner of the world. Explorers, conquistadors, slaves, and colonists brought with them ingredients to make familiar meals in their new, unfamiliar home. And in relatively short order, these foreign foods replaced our indigenous, prodigious, and delicious flavors.

Of course, other world cuisines borrow heavily from foreign ingredients, too. What would Italian cuisine be without tomatoes? Or Thai cuisine without chilies? (Both the tomato and the chili pepper are native to Mesoamerica.) The difference is that these cuisines are fusions of introduced *and* indigenous foods. These nations love their newfound flavors as if they were their own, but they are most proud of their original produce. But in America, we've ditched our biological flavors in favor of the adopted members of our food family. And it is plainly evident wherever one lives.

For example, grocery stores across the country stock the relatively insipid English walnut instead of our intensely aromatic white walnuts or our earthy black walnuts. We buy pineapples and papayas instead of pawpaws—our nation's largest native fruit with beguiling flavors of mango, banana, and vanilla cream.

Japanese persimmons—both fuyu and hachiya—are preferred over American persimmons, though ours are more plentiful and every bit as sweet. Farmed Atlantic salmon from Norway often nudges out our more flavorful (and healthful) wild Pacific salmon. Meat from our native elk and bison is leaner and more boldly flavored than cattle, yet our steaks, roasts, and burgers are almost exclusively made from beef. We tout the nutrition of exotic berries like acai and goji, but salal and huckleberry in the Pacific Northwest forests are likely as healthful and don't need to be harvested from ecologically fragile environments and then transported halfway around the world. Oregon truffles—though different in flavor and aroma than the revered Périgord and Alba truffles of France and Italy—are as magical in their own right in their own dishes.

And on the story goes. All sorts of nuts, fruits, fungi, vegetables, tubers, and proteins born from American soil and sea have for one reason or another been scratched from the American

Oyster crates, Olympia.

diet. I had to wonder, "Is American cuisine really American if it doesn't make liberal use of its very own flavors?"

I should note that our cuisine isn't the only one suffering an identity crisis. Some Australians grieve their loss of unique, indigenous flavors as well. For Ben Shewry, a gifted young chef who heads Attica restaurant in Melbourne, a single dish changed his attitude toward his nation's cuisine. Shewry explained, "When I looked at a restaurant and I saw risotto on the menu, it didn't invoke a sense of Australia in me." And that's one reason Chef Shewry decided to work with native Australian flavors, even though he admits "most people hadn't heard of 99.9 percent of these ingredients." As one restaurant critic observed, "Lamb, chicken, pork, and beef haven't made major appearances on the Attica menu for some time now." Instead, Chef Shewry reintroduces diners to native nuts like bunya bunya. Marron, the large, sweet Australian crayfish is a menu mainstay. The beef, pork, and chicken that have been absent from Attica were replaced with kangaroo, wallaby, and emu. Chef Shewry's culinary philosophy is deeply rooted in native ingredients because he believes they are an important part of Australia's heritage and something Australians should take pride in.

Chef Shewry admits acceptance of his culinary philosophy was slow. His menu was seen by some as a hurdle to garnering a following. But Shewry was steadfast, because he knew diners desired, at some level, a tangible connection to their landscape and their heritage. "The connection to your roots is one of the most important connections of all," Shewry said. And he was right. In 2017 Attica ranked thirty-second in the prestigious *The World's Best 50 Restaurants* listing. Now, top chefs from around the globe fly to Melbourne to sample true Australian cuisine, to be inspired by a pantry of unique flavors, and to learn from Attica's brilliant cook.

Back in the States, American food provocateur and Michelin-starred chef Dan Barber echoes Shewry's sentiments. Chef Barber (whose restaurant Blue Hill at Stone Barns also made the 2017 *World's Best 50* list, ranking eleventh) argues that "losing indigenous crops didn't just change what people ate; it compromised people's cultural identities." But Barber isn't content letting his food do the talking, as persuasive as it is. His critically acclaimed book *The Third Plate* is a treatise on the future of our food and an acerbic critique of today's American cuisine. He believes Manifest Destiny hurt both our cuisine and our landscape. Our land suffered, Barber contends, precisely because "settlers imposed their dietary preferences on the ecology." During this westward march, the settlers' preferences in flavor diminished ecological, and thus culinary, diversity—which Chef Barber contends is the foundation of good food. "The challenge of making delicious use of various ingredients is at the heart of all great cuisines, and it evolved from diversity," Barber writes. "Cuisines did not develop from what the land offered, as is often said; they developed from what the land demanded. The Green Revolution turned this equation on its head by making diversity expensive. It empowered only a few crops. And in the process, it dumbed down cuisine."*

I want to take a moment to help illustrate Chef Barber's argument, because it goes right to the core of the many concerns chefs, critics, and journalists have with American food today. I'll use tomatoes to make my point. Americans prize tomatoes, and we grow them everywhere in the country, even in states like Wisconsin. The issue isn't whether Wisconsinites can grow good tomatoes—they can. The issue is, tomatoes aren't well suited to Wisconsin. To grow a tomato in Wisconsin requires an abundance of human help. Seeds are germinated indoors

---

* The Green Revolution refers to research and technological initiatives occurring after World War II that boosted agricultural production here in the United States and abroad. These initiatives increased deployment of technologies such as high-yielding varieties of cereal grains; chemical fertilizers and agro-chemicals; irrigation; and mechanized cultivation.

during the latter days of winter using overhead lamps and soil warmers. Seedlings are then transplanted into cold frames during the early spring and fed copious amounts of fertilizers throughout the growing season. Pesticides—either organic or conventional—are often necessary to keep yields high and fruits blemish free. The vines are then given supplemental water in midsummer when temperatures soar and rainfall diminishes in the Upper Midwest. In the end, the Wisconsinite has raised a fabulous tomato. But at what cost?

Indigenous foods, on the other hand, require little human assistance, if any. They hatch, birth, or sprout and then grow without want for supplemental resources. Why? Because they are integral to the natural order of things; they are part and parcel of the complex biota that Mother Nature tends and keeps in perfect balance. Best of all, these foods are special to their locale. I've eaten homegrown Cherokee Purple tomatoes in Wisconsin and California and even Cherokee, North Carolina; frankly, I can't tell the difference. But I knew once I plucked my first salal berry from a thicket in the mountains along the Oregon coast that I was not going to taste its heady flavors of Concord grape, blueberry, and black plum anywhere else in the country. And no heat lamps, fertilizers, pesticides, or irrigation were needed to grow that fruit.

The best way of getting back to the rich diversity of foods that Barber and Shewry pine for is by embracing the flavors our landscape gives us, region by region. I discovered this first-hand a few years ago, eating my way through Appalachia as research for my last book. I met cooks, foragers, farmers, and food festival organizers touting the incomparable flavors of their ecologically rich environment. During my research, I came across an article by Hsiao-Ching Chou—the former food editor for the now defunct *Seattle Post Intelligencer*—who wistfully yearned for such gastronomic opportunity. Chou was on the lookout for what she called "satellites" of American cuisine, something reflective of the microregion. "When I lived in Denver," she wrote, "the challenge was to figure out what the chefs meant when they described their food as 'Rocky Mountain' or 'alpine' cuisine." Around that same time, she also discovered a burgeoning Tennessee foothills cuisine, as well as Floribbean fare. In Seattle, Chou was reporting on a restaurant owner who was championing an Olympic Peninsula cuisine—cooking that took advantage of the indigenous Dungeness crab, Olympia oysters, razor clams, geoduck, as well as locally grown fruits and vegetables. This excited Chou. "I would like to travel a mere two hours and taste foods that are familiar and yet different."

Chou highlights just one of the many reasons epicures might want to rediscover our native flavors. For her, native flavors are provocative. "It's the microregional cuisines that churn those wheels in my mind," she wrote. Barber sees great environmental benefit by getting away from our current sources of food and food production and embracing those ingredients Mother Nature provides. Shewry sees native flavors reinforcing cultural identity by connecting diners to their roots.

Perhaps the best reason to acquaint our palates with our native regional fare is the simplest: joy. There is great thrill to be had by discovering a landscape through food. Such pleasure was deftly encapsulated by American journalist Frank Bruni, the former restaurant critic for the *New York Times*. In an ode to the wondrous flavors of Puget Sound, Bruni wrote he was "hard-pressed to think of another corner or patch of the United States where the locavore sensibilities of the moment are on such florid (and often sweetly funny) display, or where they pay richer dividends, at least if you're a lover of fish." Bruni then boldly declared "To eat in and around Seattle isn't merely to eat well. It is to experience something that even many larger, more gastronomically celebrated cities and regions can't offer, not to this degree: a profound and exhilarating sense of place."

And so I motored up Interstate 5 from Sacramento to Eugene, Portland, Olympia, and Seattle—to taste what Bruni tasted and to think like Chou thought. I wanted to witness first-hand these "locavore sensibilities" and how the many landscapes of America might be healthier and happier if we ate more like the folks in the upper-left corner of our country. And I wanted to be inspired by their deep connection to their roots through food. Indeed, the reasons I wanted to eat the Pacific Northwest were many . . . including one other, rather selfish one.

I am envious of the Archaic Indian. I need to add diversity to my own diet and bolster my food list with indigenous ingredients—real American food. I can't be outdone by someone eight thousand years before my time. *I'm gaining ground on you, prehistoric American settler. Here I come!*

Introduction

WHAT IS THE PACIFIC NORTHWEST?

The Columbia River Gorge as seen from Cape Horn along the Lewis and Clark Highway.

◇◇◇◇◇◇◇◇◇◇◇◇◇◇◇◇◇◇

I became fascinated with the flavors of the Pacific Northwest during my very first visit to Seattle. And then again on my first trip to Portland. I don't remember much about either vacation; both occurred almost two decades ago. I remember making the usual tourist rounds, and I recall walking an awful lot, marveling at the casual, laid-back nature of both communities. But nothing terribly clear remains in my memory except the food. *That* remains fresh in my mind.

The dish in Seattle that did it for me couldn't have been simpler—just scrambled eggs but with one unique addition. The sight of my plate was a wee underwhelming, I'll admit. I'm not sure what I expected, but it appeared the cooks lightly poached a salmon fillet and folded some of the meat into the eggs right before serving. Nothing elaborate or froufrou; just a typical breakfast ordinary folk in the Emerald City would eat. Except the salmon was so fresh! It wasn't brined salmon (lox) or smoked salmon. It was fresh salmon, as in "brought-to-the-dock-that morning" fresh. Until that meal, I had no idea how well salmon paired with eggs. Nor had I any clue how delicious salmon could be.

My dinner in Portland was almost as modest, although in a more highbrow setting. I was at Caprial Pence's bistro across the Willamette River from downtown, and I ordered an egg-noodle dish with a wild mushroom ragout. But oh the flavor! And it wasn't just chanterelles in the ragout—which I've had plenty of in California—but a multitude of mushrooms, like morel, lobster, and pieces of bolete and shavings of truffle along with the chanterelles. The forest floor was alive and present on my plate, and boy howdy was it tasty!

Seattle is wondrously watery, and Portland delightfully earthy. Yet in those two meals, as distinct as they were, I felt I was eating produce from a communal landscape. Maybe because I was an outsider I couldn't discern the differences between the cultures and ecologies of Seattle and Portland. Seattleites tell me they associate more closely with Vancouverites than with Portlanders. Puget Sound is nothing like the Willamette-Columbia River confluence, they say. And I suppose they are right. Still, there seemed something strikingly common to both areas.

Since my trips to Seattle and Portland, I've visited southern Idaho, western Montana, and Kamloops, British Columbia. I loved the wine in Kamloops and the potatoes in Idaho, and the beef in Montana was good, too. None of these geographies, I felt, had anything obvious in common. And they certainly didn't feel connected to coastal Oregon and Washington. Yet, consult any map of the Pacific Northwest, and you will likely see a territory encompassing all of British Columbia, most of Idaho, and the western edge of Montana, along with Oregon and Washington. Some cartographers extend the boundary as far north as Alaska, south to California, and east to the Continental Divide. There doesn't seem to be as universally recognized a definition of the Pacific Northwest as there is for, say, New England or the Deep South. Even Pacific Northwesterners—when asked to draw a line—can't agree on their limits of home.

This troubled me when I began writing. I wanted to celebrate a precise geography. I was excited about this unique corner of our country that is so ecologically rich and culinarily flavorful it stands apart from anywhere else in the United States. I wanted

Mount Rainier and the Cascades inspires Tacoma's skyline.

to share my enthusiasm with the world and inspire foodies to board a plane or hop in the car and come taste this region. Not just Seattle—all of Puget Sound. And not just Portland, but the entire Willamette Valley. I wanted folks to taste the mountain berries in both the Cascades and the Coast Ranges. I wanted their breaths stolen, as mine was, by the sight of the Columbia River Gorge and the Olympic Peninsula. Each of these landscapes is unique, but they are all clearly tied together by climate, water, flora and fauna. But what is the name of this region? "Pacific Northwest" seemed the correct label, at least in my mind. But the drawn maps said otherwise.

MY PACIFIC NORTHWEST IS SPECIAL

When I ask folks what immediately comes to mind when they hear "Pacific Northwest," their mental maps depict a much smaller and far more consistent geography than what cartographers draw. The landscape we universally conjure, regardless if we are from the East Coast, the Midwest, or West Coast, is sylvan, evergreen, and damp. Our minds recall big cities—Seattle, Portland, Vancouver—and monumental icons of topography—Mount Rainier, Mount Hood, Whistler. And we all think of water, be it a river, a sound, a strait, or that which falls from the sky. The name of the region itself—Pacific Northwest—implies that the Earth's largest body of water is quite near, and that its influence on the climate and on those who live here is clearly evident.

Ecologists have a name for this distinct piece of terrain. The Pacific coast temperate rainforest is a unique ecoregion and is the largest temperate rainforest in the world. It is rich in diversity, plant and animal. Animals range from terrestrial to freshwater to marine. Some species—like salmon—are anadromous, starting and ending life in freshwater streams and rivers but spending most of it in the open sea. Shellfish, like mussels and clams

The Pacific coast temperate rainforest—shown here at Lummi Island in Washington—often grows right up to the ocean's edge.

and oysters and crabs, flourish along the tidal edge, sometimes under water, sometimes on land. The trees are hosts to some of the tastiest mushrooms and truffles in the world, while shrubs yield a dizzying array of berries: fantastically colorful gumdrops of the bramble. All of this is possible because rainforests, be they tropical or temperate, are special ecosystems incomparably conducive to life.

My college dorm mate John Morse, who works for a big software company in Redmond, Washington (you may know it), describes the PNW as a place "where dense forests wash across steep hills, and the trees are tossed by fishmongers from a dark sea up to the arms of Mount Baker, the Great White Watcher." (He majored in English, in case you were wondering.) The concise region John describes is one we all conjure when we think of the Pacific Northwest: that narrow band of terrain bounded on the east by the snow-covered peaks of the Cascade Range, the west by the Pacific Ocean, stretching from southern Oregon all the way to the 49th parallel and beyond.

And so this book will focus on that particular piece of the Pacific Northwest. I don't mean to alienate the citizens of Missoula, Boise, or even Spokane, especially if you consider yourself tried and true Pacific Northwesterners. I have visited the high deserts of the Columbia Plateau and they are stunning. No doubt the flavors in these eastern locales of the PNW are distinct and delicious, too.

But the generally accepted heart of the Pacific Northwest culture and landscape lie at the northernmost and westernmost edges of our country: where the redwoods of California peter out and Douglas fir and western red cedar take over; where mountains aren't merely granitic peaks, but volcanoes of hardened lava piercing the stratosphere; where rivers, tides, straits, and sounds abound and surround. This is the landscape that epitomizes the Pacific Northwest in the United States. And this is the PNW's best stocked larder.

1

Eugene:
BLISS FOOD

Oregon black and white truffles.

◇◇◇◇◇◇◇◇◇◇◇◇◇◇◇◇

To love truffles is to revel in contrast. White or black? European or American? Infused or shaved? Pigs or dogs? Just an earthborne fungus or the most nuanced, enchanting, provocative, exalted food on Earth?

You may already be quite familiar with truffles, those decadent black Périgords from France or the luxurious Italian whites from Alba; the fungi that the famed gastronome Jean Anthelme Brillat-Savarin once claimed were "the diamonds of the kitchen." If so, then you can appreciate their ethereal aromas and euphoric flavor (and stratospheric prices)—but I learned something that might rock your gustatory world. I discovered something better growing in the dense, coastal, evergreen forests of Oregon. And aside from a handful of locals (and maybe Sasquatch) nobody knows about these hidden treasures . . . and they just may incite Oregon's next Gold Rush.

Regardless of established French and Italian renown, let me declare with confidence that the Willamette Valley is one of the world's best truffle regions. But this shouldn't come as much surprise. America is maturing gastronomically. Our wines have bested France's most vaunted, time and again. We are excelling in craft beer, cheese, and charcuterie, and Americans now roast the best coffee and cacao beans in the world. Indeed, we have mastered many techniques in creating the finest drinks and foodstuffs gourmands have ever known. And now, we might also possess one of gastronomy's finest raw materials.

I will concede, I'm somewhat new to truffles. I had just started to delve into the mystique of these culinary gems when I came across a food celebration in the Pacific Northwest that piqued my interest, the Oregon Truffle Festival. This food festival is unique for a few reasons, one being that it is so popular. I can't recall any other multiday foodie jubilee that is held over two weekends in two different cities. The Oregon Truffle Festival, or OTF, is a concise and casual affair in and around Portland one weekend, and then a pull-out-all-the-stops extravaganza in Eugene during another. This celebration is also different in that it is held in the dead of winter. January seemed an odd month for fresh food revelry, but then again, no better way to kick-start the new year than with a food festival of unparalleled decadence. Besides, Mother Nature doesn't cater to our convenience; when She says the food is ready to eat, then eat we shall. And for Oregon truffles, that means winter.

The festival is also unique because of the diversity of guests it attracts: culinary artisans as well as scientists, locals and international visitors, jet-setting gourmands in natty attire alongside salt-of-the-earth growers donning flannel, denim, and muddy footwear. But the most conspicuous demographic amid the somewhat posh interior of the Eugene Hilton are those dressed in collars and fur coats: the shepherds, pointers, hounds, and retrievers.

THE TRUFFLE DOCTOR IS IN

I pulled into downtown Eugene and the weather was perfectly stereotypical for this time of year: cold, wet, and dreary. I checked into the hotel and then immediately sought one of the large conference rooms. I don't usually attend food festivals carrying an attaché with notepads and reference materials and an audio recorder, but I had been told this first day of the festival was going to be a heady affair; not in a gastronomical sense but an intellectual one.

I walked into the conference and took an aisle seat next to a red-haired retriever lying contently on the floor. Dr. Charles Lefevre had just finished his introductory remarks, acknowledging the list of distinguished speakers here today, though Lefevre is quite distinguished himself; well-known among truffle scientists and growers throughout the world. Two years before Charles completed his doctorate in forest mycology at Oregon State, a grower from Corvallis asked him if he could inoculate hazelnut seedlings with *Tuber melanosporum*—the delicious fungus gourmands know better as the French black truffle, or Périgord. Charles succeeded, which garnered the attention of the *Los Angeles Times*, thrusting him into the public spotlight. After the media splash that there might soon be a Périgord orchard on the West Coast, demand for truffle-inoculated saplings surged, and Lefevre founded New World Truffieres, a company that produces inoculated trees for truffle orchards throughout North

America. The excitement continued to build. Soon Lefevre's promising work was featured in the *New Yorker*, the *New York Times*, *Discovery Channel*, *Forbes*, *Audubon*, *Smithsonian*, and other notable periodicals.

Dr. Charles Lefevre inspects one of his recently inoculated saplings at the Oregon Truffle Festival.

There was good reason to be excited over US-grown Périgords, but Charles believed our native truffles should be equally illustrious. In 2006, he and his wife, Leslie Scott, founded the Oregon Truffle Festival—the first truffle festival of its kind outside of Europe. It was to be more than a boisterous celebration of those delectable French and Italian fungi, however. The founding of the OTF was rooted in science and education, as a participatory event that could help grow the burgeoning truffle cultivation industry in North America through symposia, led by the brightest minds in botany, forest ecology, and mycology. But it was also an opportunity for Charles and Leslie to showcase the specialness of Oregon truffles.

Today, at the Truffle Growers Forum, Lefevre's invited guests were going to expound on truffle culture, sharing trials and insights of cultivating truffles in their respective corners of the world: Japan, Australia, Canada, and Spain. This was going to be a serious day of discussion—because there is serious money to made with truffles.

For a truffle newbie like myself, there were numerous nuggets of information to be gleaned from these expert discussions. I had already known that a truffle is the fruiting body of a fungus that lives in symbiosis with tree roots. The fungus explores the soil for water and minerals, which it passes along to the tree. In exchange, the tree provides sugars produced through photosynthesis to the fungus. Many tree species can serve as hosts for European truffles, and the most common are oak and hazelnut, but also chestnut, elm, beech, and poplar.

What I didn't know is that, in the Willamette Valley, there is just *one* tree that the native truffles latch onto, the coast Douglas fir, the state tree of Oregon. Since the coast Douglas fir's range is compact and delimited—it grows only in that narrow band of the Pacific coast temperate rainforest between Vancouver Island and Northern California, and west of the Cascades to the Pacific Ocean—Oregon truffles are a distinct, place-based delicacy.

One of the panel discussions focused on truffle aroma and the science behind those captivating smells. Dr. Lefevre was joined by Harold McGee an American author famous for his work on the chemistry of food science and cookery. McGee's seminal book, *On Food and Cooking*, influenced some of the world's top culinary talent, including NYC's Daniel Boulud and Britain's Heston Blumenthal. Alton Brown describes McGee's book as "the Rosetta stone of the culinary world."

McGee was contrasting the aromas of Oregon white truffles with those luxurious ones from Alba, Italy. "Other than a funky animal note, Oregon truffles don't bear any resemblance to Albas," he noted. "With the Italian varieties, there is a sulphur, asafetida-like smell as soon as the mushroom comes out of the ground, but not so with the Oregon whites." (Asafetida is a common spice in savory Indian cuisine, and, as the name implies, it has a fetid smell before it is cooked. It is also known as "devil's dung.") But when McGee inhales the scent of fresh Oregon white truffles, he immediately smells tropical fruit. "I get hints of pineapple, but then it's gone. Now it's more like barnyard, but that, too, is fleeting. Now it's back to exotic fruit . . . is it mango?" McGee says Oregon truffles are beguiling shapeshifters. "As soon as you recognize one thing," he says, "it morphs into the next."

McGee then posited, "Why do truffles emit these notes?" Lefevre jumped in, "Because truffles want to be found. They *need* us to like them."

◇◇◇◇◇◇◇◇◇◇◇◇◇◇◇◇◇

Mycological reproduction is the reason truffles smell so amazing. Since they grow at the base of trees, under the duff, they are completely hidden from view. Unlike mushrooms, which poke above the forest floor and rely on wind to spread their spores, truffles need something to announce, "Hey, I'm down here, come find me!" So, they toss thousands of intensely aromatic compounds into the air, alluring scents that attract fungivores—forest critters that love eating mushrooms and truffles, like boars and jays and slugs, and, of course, humans. These aromatic compounds help ward off predators—bacteria and other fungi, namely—while attracting animals to ensure dissemination.

Interestingly, there aren't any poisonous truffles, as there are with mushrooms, because "there is no biological benefit of killing the thing that ensures procreation," explains Lefevre. However, some truffle varieties are vastly more aromatic than others, and thus, more appealing to us.

As a panel of experts discuss truffle reproduction at the Oregon Truffle Festival, the guests enjoy crisp potato wafers sandwiching smoked salmon roe, grilled avocado, and fresh Oregon white truffle shavings.

But there is no need to broadcast these bewitching aromas unless the truffle is mature and ready to reproduce; in other words, ripe. And this has been a ubiquitous concern for champions of Oregon truffles. "A few years ago, Oregon truffles weren't interesting; completely forgettable," recalls McGee. "But that has changed with the Oregon Truffle Festival." McGee credits Lefevre for introducing chefs and gourmands to good, *ripe* Oregon truffles. Which makes all the difference between a forgettable fungus and one that fetches hundreds of dollars per pound. "Smelling a ripe Oregon truffle can be like tasting your first ripe papaya or mango or pineapple," McGee says. "And then you realize, there's something exotic growing right under our feet!"

Any produce with which we are not familiar, whether fruit or fungus, we must learn when it is ready for harvest. Unlike tomatoes or bell peppers, truffles have no culinary value unless they are completely ripe. But truffles don't turn red to let us know when we should eat them. Instead, we must rely on aroma. Until we know what aromas we should be smelling, any unearthed truffle that lacks those heady scents might be castigated, tossed aside, and forgotten because we wrongly assumed they were inferior. Such has been the legacy of Oregon truffles; that is, until the OTF.

Though our nose is the best gauge for determining truffle ripeness, there are clues we can see. One way to tell if a truffle is ripe is to peek inside. Truffle exteriors are rough, dusky, and pimply, but inside, the fruit reminds me of the finest granite, beautifully speckled, with white venation permeating a rich buff color in the case of white truffles or a deep mocha brown in the case of black. Venation complexity and clarity improves as the fruit ripens. To determine when a truffle is ripe, take a pocketknife, flick off a pimple, and look for contrast. When the browns are dark and the white veins are stark and clear—no blurring or muddying—the truffle is ready.

We can also rely on our sense of sight (and touch) when determining if a truffle has peaked and is starting to decay. Charles says recognizing this trait is the most important, because a truffle will continue to improve—ripen—even when those veins are clear. Think about persimmons. The fruit improves dramatically while it sits on our kitchen counter. We must exercise patience and keep a watchful eye, waiting until the moment right before a persimmon starts to rot. Then, we will be rewarded with the most luscious, sweetest flavors. "You have to know that moment when a truffle dies," Charles impresses upon the audience. "Once it starts to sweat and soften, that's the hallmark your truffle is dead."

◇◇◇◇◇◇◇◇◇◇◇◇◇◇◇◇◇◇◇◇

When a truffle is ripe and releases its aromas into the air, there is some debate as to what, exactly, the fungivore is attracted.

Do these compounds simply smell good, stimulating appetite? Or do these compounds stimulate something else in our body, unrelated to hunger? Recent research suggests possibly the latter. Black truffles produce anandamide, a compound that prompts the release of mood-elevating chemicals in the brain using the same biological mechanism as tetrahydrocannabinol, or THC, the principal psychoactive constituent in marijuana. *Scientific American* cited a recent study in Italy in which researchers noted that black truffles produce anandamides to control melanin synthesis—pigmentation of the truffle's skin—but that they may also have another function. The research team believes anandamides may have evolved as a signal that makes pigs, dogs, humans, and other truffle-eating animals search for them. When fungivores locate and eat these ripe truffles, they literally find themselves in hog heaven from anandamide intoxication. The desire of mammals to get high helps ensure ripe truffles are found and their spores are spread far and wide, thereby improving chances of reproduction.

Anandamides play a role in enhancing mood while diminishing memory, pain, and depression. For this reason, some scientists refer to anandamide as "the bliss molecule." (Anandamide comes from the Sanskrit word *ananda*, meaning joy, or bliss.)

I asked Harold McGee his opinion about anandamides and about this sense of bliss some feel after gorging on truffles. He said he hasn't studied it, but his first impression is it is likely hype. "I think it's psychosomatic," McGee said. "With the lore and the mystique of truffles, and their exorbitant price, people want to believe this stuff; it adds to truffles' charm."

But Charles and I disagreed. While I don't have the scientific background to persuasively argue my point to McGee, I do have experience.

At my first visit to the Oregon Truffle Festival, I most certainly felt a calm euphoria wash over me almost immediately after each meal. The dose might have something to do with the feeling; never have I eaten so much fresh truffle in one sitting. But the mental and physiological effect it had on me was quite similar to what I experience after eating Indian cuisine. Whenever I eat a large East Indian meal, one with a variety of curries, I feel that same bliss I felt after eating truffles, a deeply contented stupor. It never lasts long; maybe a few minutes. It is a distinct feeling from the one many of us experience after feasting on turkey for Thanksgiving. I'm not sure of the reason, but I do know that the unique cocktail of coriander, cardamom, cumin, asafetida, and turmeric reacts with my bodily chemistry and alters my mood in a very positive, desirable way. And it seems truffles do the same. Regardless of the explanation, I return to Indian cuisine and truffles time and again, because I find them both delicious and pleasurable. Those intoxicating, heady flavors—in curries and truffles—feed both my belly and my head.

THE JORIAD

The crowd was hushed inside the Lane County Livestock Arena, and the atmosphere thick with excitement. Marcy Tippman and other competitors sat nervously with their BFFs—best furried friends—watching as the competition trotted and sniffed, searching the paddock for that unmistakable truffle scent.

Charles Lefevre was on the sidelines watching eagerly to see which canine would impress this year at the third annual North American Truffle Dog Championship, also known as the Joriad. This competition quickly has become one of the signature events at the Oregon Truffle Festival, and for Charles the Joriad is a source of pride and accomplishment. He knows that someday, these dogs will help convince the world's most distinguished palates that Oregon truffles are as precious as those European "diamonds of the kitchen."

I walked over to Charles and we spoke a bit about the competition. He told me the Joriad was named in honor of Jory,

Oregon's unique and official state soil. Jory soil, named after Jory Hill in Marion County, is a deep, well-draining, exceptionally productive layer of earth that forms the foothills flanking the Willamette Valley. Underneath its rich layer of humus are strata of dark reddish-brown loams and clays that support a diversity of forest plants, most notably berry bushes of all sorts, hazelnuts, Christmas trees, and the coast Douglas fir—the host tree for native Oregon truffles.

Charles shared with me how the Oregon Truffle Festival came to be; he said the idea started in his refrigerator. Charles understood why many chefs and gourmands considered Oregon truffles inferior, inexpensive substitutes for the real thing. But he knew that at times Oregon truffles could be great. He would pull truffles from his refrigerator—European as well as Oregonian—and smell them side by side. He found some of the Oregon truffles were every bit as heady and nuanced as the European ones, but others were flat. The aroma was inconsistent. He then discovered the reason for the inconsistency; his Oregon truffles had been harvested by a rake.

◇◇◇◇◇◇◇◇◇◇◇◇◇◇◇◇◇◇

You might have heard about pigs rooting around the grounds of Piedmont, Italy, digging up gorgeous white truffles that gourmands go gaga over; fungi that can sell for $2,000 per pound. It is a romantic, if not medieval image, though quite real and contemporary. Like humans, pigs love truffles. The truffle forager searching for fungus with his sow in tow must be quick and strong, however. Once the swine dips its nose in the duff, its snout rooting for that perfectly ripe truffle—then finding it—it becomes an every-mammal-for-itself struggle. The pig attempts to gobble down its newfound prize while the human muscles his two-hundred-pound pet aside, keeping it at bay with one arm while the other cuts the truffles free from the tree roots.

Pigs were historically used to hunt truffles because of their acute sense of smell and an affinity for rooting in the dirt. Best of all, pigs have an inherent attraction to the fungus. Truffles produce an aromatic compound similar to a sex pheromone found in boar saliva, a scent to which the sow is drawn. Sure, pigs make excellent truffle hunters, but not if your prized fungi are eaten before you get even a whiff. Not only that, but rooting pigs destroy sensitive mycelia, the fungus strands that would have eventually produced more truffles. Pigs are so destructive to forest habitat that, even after centuries of romantic tradition, Italy banned their use in truffle hunting.

Instead of pigs, truffle hunters often take to rakes. Our noses are not as sensitive as a pig's, but raking can make up for that handicap. And raking for truffles is quite efficient. Just take a jaunt into the woods, drop your rake into the duff, and start raking the forest floor until you unearth your prize. Raking can yield enormous hauls of fresh truffles—but it has a significant downside. Raking can damage the truffles and the sensitive ecosystem they need to produce more.

When a rake is used to unearth truffles, the tines can gouge the skins of the subterranean fungus, even slicing them open or breaking them completely. This allows those alluring gases to rapidly escape while hastening decomposition. Additionally, raking is no better for the environment than rooting pigs. Some truffles grow in soil more than a foot deep. Raking to this depth severs young host roots, destroys truffle mycelia, and alters those unique Jory soil profiles, drastically reducing future harvests.

And rakes are indiscriminate, harvesting all the truffles, mature as well as juvenile. The raker has no idea if a truffle is ripe or not until after it has been harvested. In this way, raking truffles is akin to seine netting salmon. A seine ensnares a whole school of fish, some maybe too young to be harvested. The rake does the same. This is why Lefevre found some of his truffles were intensely aromatic, while others were flat. He had, in his refrigerator, a few ripe truffles, but a bunch of immature ones as well.

◇◇◇◇◇◇◇◇◇◇◇◇◇◇◇◇◇◇◇

When a truffle purveyor tells you his or her truffles were "dog harvested," it's the equivalent of the farmer saying his tomatoes are organic. It's a point of distinction that has a lot of cachet among truffle cognoscenti, because it means the truffles were sensitively and sustainably procured. Dogs have a keen sense of smell but, unlike pigs, they aren't so keen on truffle flavor. And they only sniff out the ripe truffles, so it's a win all around. Immature truffles are left to grow below ground, and there's no contest between the animal and the human for the ripe truffle. The dog merely points to the truffle, steps aside, and awaits a treat from its master's pocket.

When the OTF began in 2006, Lefevre noted there weren't any truffle dogs in the western United States. He then met Jim Sanford, a dog trainer at the posh Blackberry Farm resort in the Smoky Mountain foothills of Tennessee. Sanford had spent two decades traveling the world and training elephants before settling in Tennessee. He started working the front desk at Blackberry Farm, then became the resort's first fly-fishing instructor. Sanford then started Blackberry's horseback program, and now trains truffle dogs for the resort.

Sanford trains Lagotto Romagnolo pups, a breed of gundog from northern Italy originally used to retrieve waterfowl. The Lagotto Romagnolo (*lag-OH-toe ro-man-YO-lo*) is a smallish breed with floppy ears, thick curls of fur, and a happy, bright disposition. Lagotti are easily trained and have an acute sense of smell, making them the ideal dog to assist the Romagnolo in their search for their beloved truffles. Of course, most all dogs have a keen sense of smell, but some are best at tracking down foxes (foxhounds and beagles), pheasants (German short-haired pointers and Brittany spaniels), or narcotics, bombs, and bad guys (German shepherds and rottweilers). Lagotti happen to possess a deftness for sniffing out subterranean fungus, and those who love truffles consider them the preeminent dog for hunting such delicacies.

Mossimo, a Lagotto Romagnolo, sniffed out a truffle in the woods outside Eugene, to the delight of his owner and us spectators.

◇◇◇◇◇◇◇◇◇◇◇◇◇◇◇◇◇◇

Back at the livestock arena, Lagotti were certainly the most represented of any breed in the Joriad. But there were other breeds you might suspect could give Lagotti a run for their money: a spaniel and a pointer, a couple of hounds and retrievers, and a few shepherds, including a gorgeous and fit German shepherd named Cowboy.

But Marcy Tippmann's canine is a crowd favorite, because everyone roots for an underdog. And this dog can get under a lot of things, since its stature is all of eleven inches. Gustave is a Chihuahua mix and looks more like a leashed rat chasing cheese in this horse paddock than a well-heeled hunting dog retrieving gourmet food. But Gustave is no slouch.

Marcy told me she started training Gustave with a fifteen dollar bottle of Oregon truffle oil and a two dollar clicker. She began by placing three jars on the floor, each stuffed with a cotton ball, but only one sprinkled with truffle oil. Each time Gustave sniffed the correct jar, he was rewarded with a click and a treat.

The games became more challenging for Gustave: the truffled cotton balls were moved under a blanket, then throughout the house, and eventually outside. "What I love most about truffle training is how much my dog loves it," Marcy said. "When I get home from work on a dark and rainy winter night, we get to play his favorite game—he gets to run around and sniff, and gets treats and praise for doing it, and I don't have to leave the house!"

As Gustave got more proficient and the weather improved, Marcy would sprinkle truffle oil on dog treats and go out into the dark, casting them blindly. Neither Gustave nor Marcy knew where the truffle-scented treats would land. Soon, it was time for a true truffle hunt.

It was an exciting moment when Gustave made the leap from sniffing out a truffle-scented object in a controlled environment to finding the real thing in the forest. "I could practically hear the wheels turning in his little head," Marcy said. "Ohhhh, this is what we have been looking for!" Gustave was now ready for the Joriad.

Gustave was off to a quick start, finding three truffle-scented targets in quick succession. But the final two eluded him. There was just too much ground for those little legs to traverse, and Gustave ran out of time. Alas, Gustave didn't make it to finals. Cowboy, that fine-looking German shepherd, fared best in the

Gustave pulls Marcy Tippmann in his search for truffle-scented targets.

preliminary rounds, and he and the other top finishers advanced to the main event: hunting real truffles deep in the woods of Lane County.

Still, Gustave fared admirably. Listening to Marcy speak of Gustave, you can't help but share in her pride, especially in a field of competitors bred for truffle hunting. She told me, "You know, he's a real dog, just very small . . . and I am very proud of him."

Marcy said she learned a lot about dogs and truffles when competing in the Joriad, and made some friends, too. Cowboy's owner invited Tippman and Gustave up to Seattle to go truffle hunting together. "It was such a great experience," Marcy said, speaking of the event. "I was nervous that the other contestants would resemble the ultracompetitive characters from the movie *Best in Show*, but everyone I talked to was kind and excited to be there."

◇◇◇◇◇◇◇◇◇◇◇◇◇◇◇◇◇◇◇

If you're a dog owner and wondering if your BFF might have potential to track down those prized forest fungi, Marcy has some encouraging advice. "Truffle hunting is not an elite activity," she says. "You don't need a dog that costs thousands of dollars, expensive training materials, or a professional dog trainer. All you need is a scent to search for, a dog who is willing to please, time, patience, and enthusiasm."

Tippmann's advice proved sage the following year. Gustave returned to the Joriad in 2018, bent on finding all five of the truffle-scented objects buried in that livestock arena. He needed every second, but as the buzzer sounded, Gustave stopped, pointed, and Marcy quickly unearthed the fifth and final faux-truffle, lifting it high above her head in exaltation. Gustave had advanced to the finals.

Searching for truffle-scented objects in a controlled environment is one thing, but the real challenge lay ahead. Gustave would now have to compete against all of the finalists simultaneously, searching for *real* Oregon truffles in the Lane County woods. While Gustave was no longer a rookie, the odds seemed stacked against this compact-statured pooch.

When the duff had settled, the victor had sniffed out an astonishing quantity of ripe truffles: seventeen, blowing away the second-place finisher whose haul was a respectable quantity of ten. But when the winner was revealed, the audience gasped; all were shocked, including the dog's trainer. Gustave, that diminutive canine dwarfed by the competition and those towering Douglas fir trees, stood above all others that day, the preeminent truffle dog, and champion of the Joriad.

LET'S EAT! (BUT SNIFF FIRST)

We have long been told that taste is 90 percent smell, but nothing proves this adage more clearly than truffles.

I had eaten quite the envious share of these delicacies during my visits to the OTF. Paper-thin slices of perfectly ripe Oregon blacks, whites, and Périgords garnished almost every divine bite. I was curious what all these little truffle disks tasted like by themselves, without accompaniment. But each time I popped that slice into my mouth and chewed, like I would a small potato chip, the impressions were the same. There isn't much flavor directly on the tongue, and the texture can be off-putting; a bit dry and mealy. When sliced, fresh truffles have all the juice, tenderness, and flavor of cardstock. But this is certainly not a knock on truffles, as truffles aren't meant to be eaten this way.

The magic of truffles are those tens of thousands of aromatic compounds off-gassed from the ripe fruiting body. But for us to eat those gases, we need a receptacle, something that can capture and store those aromas. That receptacle is fat.

In the presence of cheese, cream, oil, eggs, and lard, truffles metamorphose, evolving from a predominantly olfactory ingredient to a treat for the tongue. A slice of truffle by itself isn't very flavorful. But it is astonishing how quickly the adjacent fat will absorb those aromatic compounds released from that truffle chip. Shave the truffle into tiny, delicate whorls, and even more aromas are transferred into the fats.

Now that we have truffle aromas infusing our food, aromas that can now be tasted, what, exactly, are we tasting? That's a good question, and one that's difficult to answer. Truffles are unlike anything you might have smelled *or* tasted. And that is why they are so revered.

If you are just getting acquainted with Oregon truffles, I have found you can employ a white or black pairing like you might employ a white or red wine pairing. Oregon white wines and white truffles marry amazingly well with shellfish, white seafood and meats (like halibut and pork), and simple egg and cheese dishes. Red meat, foie gras, rich pasta dishes with pungent herbs and copious amounts of butter and cream pair better with Oregon black truffles and red wine. Pairing Oregon truffles, and wine, with salmon can go either way. Salmon is bold and rich enough to be paired with a pinot noir and black truffles, but also works well with the lighter aromas and flavors of Oregon white truffles and pinot gris, for example. Ditto for pâté. Leslie Scott, the cofounder of the OTF, generally concurs with these pairing tips, but her nose and palate are more deft than mine. "White truffles are light and can certainly have fruity notes," she says. "Some say apricot or citrus, but subtle, on the edge of that volatile, indescribable acetone thing they have going on." Leslie says Oregon whites are divine with myriad shellfish, like scallops and Dungeness crab, but also any roe as well. She also highlights pork, especially charcuterie, as a stunning mate to Oregon whites. "Elias Cairo of Olympia Provisions is making absolutely beautiful salumi with them, as well as pâtés," she says. But Leslie's favorite dishes pair Oregon white truffles with simple fare, like a potato gratin, or an utterly sublime potato and cod dish that Seattle chef Renee Erickson prepared at the Grand Truffle Dinner in 2017.

"But Oregon black truffles may be the most complex truffles on the planet," Scott says, "and it is their huge versatility that I think gives them an edge over any other black truffle I have had." She notes that their flavor profile changes as they ripen, and those that are well handled and harvested just at the beginning of ripeness can offer chefs innumerable opportunities to showcase Oregon black truffles in a variety of dishes. Just hearing Scott's description would make any foodie salivate for a taste of this fungus: "There's definitely tropical fruit at the outset—mango, pineapple, banana—these are the most common—to cheesy chocolatey funk, to really meaty on the edge of rot, which do amazing things with red meats." She also says Oregon black truffles are "magical under the skin of poultry, in fois gras, in desserts, and salad dressings."

Because truffle aromas and flavors are so nuanced and often fleeting, impressions vary, and so do the opinions of which varieties are best suited to different proteins and fats. Charles Ruff, the OTF's culinary director, says he thinks first about how the truffle will be used or presented in a dish. "What I mean is that depending on the dish, one truffle may show better based on the method of execution," he says. "There are ways to capture and integrate the flavor and aromas of white truffles that are just not as effective with the blacks." Ruff says black truffles tend to be more delicate, both in aroma and heat resistance. "When it comes to flavor, the black packs a wallop, but how you capture and present that punch is the trick."

Ruff tries to pair Oregon blacks with dishes that typically have fewer ingredients and less challenging, competing flavors, such as cream sauces and cheese, especially if the cheese is subtle. In these dishes, he aims to have the complex flavor of black truffles punch through. As Scott noted, Oregon black truffles are extremely versatile. Though she and I prefer Oregon whites with light, white fish, Ruff loves to pair black truffles with Oregon black cod "cooked only in a warm black truffle broth and finished

In the kitchen at the Eugene Hilton, a chef shaves fresh Oregon black truffle over chou farci—a chicken stuffed cabbage roll.

with a few slices of freshly shaved black truffle." He agrees that the blacks pair well with poultry, foie gras, and especially pork or duck based pâtés, "but they also make a stunning ice cream," he says.

One of the Oregon black truffle's most intoxicating aromas, yet one that Ruff says is scarcely cited, is almond essence. "When micro-planing a black truffle for a direct infusion in something like cream, if you turn over the micro-plane and smell the macerated flesh of the truffle, it is incredible, and the closest thing I can liken it to is an intense amaretto. . . . That aroma is what I think of when I hear people reference 'Ambrosia' or the nectar of the gods."

If the blacks are nutty, fruity, and earthy, then the whites are brassy and gassy, according to Ruff. "The brassy high notes of the whites are the first thing that hit most people, and it is literally in their face. Rather than having to unearth some of the underlying nuances of the black truffles, the whites stand up and broadcast their existence to the world." Ruff takes advantage of that brass and will often use white truffles with more flavor-forward fish (and fish parts), like salmon and halibut cheeks, because the white's flavor is assertive and remains clear. He also likes Oregon whites mated to anything with butter. "My axiom: if it is good dipped in butter, it will be even better with white truffled butter."

Ruff also points out that Oregon whites are one, if not the only, truffle that can stand up to a smoked element in dishes. Which is important when considering the cuisine of the Pacific Northwest, a region with a long history of smoking fish, especially salmon. And he says he almost always picks up some oniony, garlicky funk in ripe Oregon white truffles, much like ramps, but it's tamed by a fresh lemon thyme aroma with soft notes evocative of saffron.

Scott had pointed out that Ruff's pairings work exquisitely when the truffles are infused into a broth or a sauce, as opposed to being freshly shaved onto the dish. "Charles Ruff is a genius at truffle infusions," Scott says. "The benefit of infusions is the ability to harness the flavors and aromas to use at a later time. You have more flexibility with infusions. However," Leslie cautions, "one bad truffle can ruin the entire infusion."

Leslie recalled a gorgeous truffle dinner Charles Ruff prepared for her birthday in March. It was a sumptuous testament to Ruff's skilled hand at truffle infusions, because fresh truffles weren't in season. Still, Leslie says nothing beats a fresh, shaved truffle. "Fresh truffles are what keep truffles from being just a fad foodstuff," she says. "It's why they have such high price tags—all the magic and mystique are in the fresh truffle!"

Such is the joy of truffles. Endless hours of scintillating, titillating debate on aromas and flavors, sharing opinions and memories of dishes cooked and tasted, and reveling in the contrasts of this delectable gustatory treasure: White or black? European or Oregonian? Infused or shaved? Dog harvested? Naturally.

OREGON TRUFFLE RECIPES AND FOODSTUFFS

The Oregon Truffle Festival should top every gastronome's bucket list, because it excites the mind as well as the palate. And few things invigorate the spirit like a walk in the woods with a furry friend in search of buried, gustatory treasure.

But Sunday is a special day at the OTF for folks who love to spend time in the kitchen. This is the Fresh Truffle Marketplace, and offers just-harvested truffles, delectable truffled samples, and edible truffle education. It is an all-day affair during which vendors share truffle tips with each other as well as with the guests and talented chefs prepare simple meals showcasing the luxury and versatility of truffles. I found truffle-infused butter, ice cream, confections, salt, charcuterie and pâté; even truffle-infused fresh eggs! (The truffle aromas settle in the yolks, so poach, soft boil, or fry sunny-side up. Since truffle flavor dissipates with heat, refrain from cooking the eggs too long.) The air

A truffled salume, one of many delectable truffle-infused samples at the OTF's Fresh Truffle Marketplace.

in the room was heavily perfumed, and lines were long to taste many of these treats or to simply ogle the New World Truffieres table, where gorgeous, just-harvested Périgords and Oregon blacks sat side by side, each variety available for purchase.

One of the most common foodstuffs, as you might expect, was truffle oil. But it was also the most eye-opening. I can't recall any foodstuff changing my opinion of a particular ingredient quicker than *good* truffle oil; *real* truffle oil. I should take a moment to shed some light on this, as truffle oil had been a hotly discussed subject at the OTF.

I learned to be extremely cautious of any truffled foodstuff, but especially oil. As we witness the American palate maturing, with a good deal of the adult population now anointing themselves bona fide foodies, the market is offering flavors that have long been revered in regions where haute cuisine was born. Truffles are one of those flavors.

But beware. The overwhelming majority of truffle oil in your market is either: A) made with ghastly inferior truffles (there are several species of truffle, only a couple of which are prized); B) Infused with the desirable species of truffle, but those that were unsalable fresh because they were underripe or overripe, or else gouged or cut when harvested due to raking; or, most likely, C) flavored with 2,4-dithiapentane, one of the tens of thousands of aromatic compounds (albeit, one of the most potent) that has been isolated in a lab and added to cooking oil. Most truffle experts pooh-pooh truffle oils because they are nothing more than a Johnny one note.

Not only that, but truffle aroma turns rancid quite quickly. Most truffle oil, even if it has been infused with good quality truffles, has likely spoiled before you even have a chance to sprinkle it on your French fries. "The highest and best use of most truffle oil," says Charles Ruff, "is training dogs."

But at the OTF, this was the *Fresh* Truffle Marketplace, where culinary artisans have taken time and pride in infusing their oils (and sheep's milk cheese, pork charcuterie, organic spirits, sea salt, sweet cream butter) with only the finest, ripest Oregon truffles. And oh! What a difference that makes! Again, as scrumptious as these foodstuffs are, I need to remember that these ethereal aromas won't last long. What is pungent and fresh today will be putrid in a matter of days.

The crowd highlight of the day were the many intimate cooking demonstrations. While Saturday night's Grand Truffle Dinner showcased the amazing talent and creativity of some of the PNW's best chefs, whose dishes dazzled in their beauty, flavor, and exquisite execution, Sunday's cooking demonstrations focused on quick meals that could be readily replicated by the home cook. The dishes and bites I found most appealing were those that added decadence to familiar foods and those that paired Oregon truffles with other native PNW flavors.

Consider these recipes an introduction to Oregon truffles, both black and white. I love these recipes because they are luxurious, yet quite accessible.

TRUFFLED PECORINO CHEESE

The technique to make a decadent truffled cheese is the same for any truffled foodstuff that possesses copious amounts of fat (or alcohol). At the OTF, chicken ranchers were selling truffled eggs. Distillers sold their signature truffled vodka. The line was fantastically long for guests waiting to taste a white truffle salami. Food artisans suffused oils, butters, creams, and even mayonnaise with the heady aromas and flavors of Oregon truffles, simply by letting the fungus and the fat sit together in a covered container. It's almost inconceivable that such rich gustatory reward can be had for so little effort.

All the foodstuffs I sampled throughout the weekend were delicious, but I found cheese and truffles to be the most balanced and complementary, and I left the festival craving more. As soon as I returned home with a couple fresh Oregon black truffles in my bag, I decided to try my hand at making a truffled cheese. But which cheese to use? Surely, some must mate better with Oregon black truffles than others.

I consulted with what many *fromage*-o-philes regard to be the finest cheese shop in the Pacific Northwest. The Cheese Bar in Portland is a nationally acclaimed cheese counter with a rotating stock of some two hundred cheeses from around the world, including many from the Willamette Valley. The staff noted that great Italian cheese makers consider pecorino and black truffles the quintessential matrimony. Indeed, one of the preeminent cheeses in the world is *pecorino al tartufo*— a pecorino from Tuscany that has been studded with flakes of black truffle. Though any cheese will work, The Cheese Bar confirmed that a raw (unpasteurized), semi-firm sheep's milk cheese, like pecorino, is the perfect sponge for absorbing Oregon black truffles' almond-y, fruity, and earthy aromas.

INGREDIENTS

3–4 small Oregon black truffles, or 1 large one, quartered
8 ounce block or wedge of pecorino cheese

PREPARATION

Wrap the truffles in a paper towel to wick away moisture, then place them in a glass or ceramic casserole. Alternatively, I prefer to lay the truffles on a bed of uncooked white rice, foregoing the paper towel. Unwrap the cheese and set in the casserole with the truffles and cover. Place the covered dish in the refrigerator for up to 3 days, and upon opening, you will have something sublime.

VARIATIONS

Instead of cheese, try nestling a stick of butter in the casserole with the truffles. Or place a container filled with avocado, grapeseed, or other neutral-flavored cooking oil into the casserole dish to make your own truffle oil. Try adding your favorite *salume*—or farm fresh eggs or even duck fat—and let them imbibe the truffle's perfume.

BUTTERMILK FRIED OYSTERS WITH TRUFFLED RÉMOULADE

(Makes 16 hors d'oeuvres)

Recipe courtesy of Christian DeBenedetti and Andrea Slonecker, inspired by a similar recipe in their book, Beer Bites: Tasty Recipes and Perfect Pairings for Brew Lovers

The beverage that accompanied every truffle dish served that weekend—lunch, dinner, or happy hour nibble—was wine. And for obvious reasons. The similarities are astounding and wholly complementary, with each variety of wine and truffle yielding a heady combination of aromas and flavors, some fruity, others earthy, some subtle and fleeting, others obvious and lingering. But at the Fresh Truffle Markeplace, Christian DeBenedetti and Andrea Slonecker proved that beer can be a rightful companion to an assortment of truffled bites.

Here, these Portland-based food and beverage authors took a Louisiana favorite and gave it a PNW spin, with the use of Pacific oysters and Oregon truffles. The reason this rémoulade works so well with truffles is because Slonecker tamed the piquancy by omitting the Dijon mustard and Tabasco that are traditionally blended into this sauce. These omissions allow some of the subtler truffle flavors to be readily discernible. The endive is yet another playful bridge between PNW and creole cuisines. Endives are chicories; the roots of which are roasted and ground as a popular coffee additive in New Orleans, while those in the PNW prefer the leaves.

DeBenedetti recommends washing these yummy fritters down with a Big Ripple Belgian Tripel from Eugene's Falling Sky Brewing Co.

INGREDIENTS

Rémoulade

½ cup mayonnaise
2 tablespoons cornichons or dill pickles, minced
1 tablespoon capers, drained, rinsed, and minced
1 tablespoon fresh parsley, minced
1 tablespoon shallots, minced

1 teaspoon sherry vinegar
½ teaspoon paprika
Fine sea salt and freshly ground black pepper
2–3 Oregon white truffles (depending on size), grated and
    sliced

Oysters

1 cup fine cornmeal or corn flour
½ cup all-purpose flour
1½ teaspoons Old Bay seasoning
1 teaspoon fine sea salt, plus more for additional seasoning
1 cup buttermilk
16 small Pacific oysters, shucked
Peanut or vegetable oil for frying
3 large Belgian endives, trimmed and separated into leaves

PREPARATION

Rémoulade

Stir together the mayonnaise, cornichons, capers, parsley, shallots, vinegar, and paprika in a small bowl, then season to taste
with salt and black pepper. Stir in some grated truffle, a little
at a time, to your taste. The sauce can be served immediately,
but it is best after the truffle infuses for a few hours, or up to 3
days in the refrigerator.

Oysters

Whisk together the cornmeal, flour, Old Bay, and 1 teaspoon
salt in a shallow bowl. Pour the buttermilk into another shallow bowl. Dip the oysters one at a time in the buttermilk, and
then dredge them in the cornmeal mixture, patting gently to

help it adhere and coat evenly. Collect the breaded oysters on a wire rack as you work.

Pour oil into a large skillet to a depth of ¾ inch and heat over medium-high heat. When the oil reaches 350°F, or when a crumb of breading sizzles enthusiastically, gently add some of the oysters, being careful not to overcrowd the pan. Fry, turning once, until golden and crisp on both sides, about 2 minutes per side. Transfer the fried oysters to paper towels to drain and sprinkle with salt while still warm. Repeat to fry the remaining oysters, adjusting the heat as needed to maintain the oil temperature and allowing it to return to 350°F between batches.

To assemble, arrange the 16 largest endive leaves on a serving platter (reserve the small inner leaves for another use). Spoon a dollop of the rémoulade into the wide, cuplike end of each leaf. Nestle a fried oyster on the sauce and finish with a thin slice of white truffle. Serve immediately.

BLACK TRUFFLE PASTA WITH MARSALA CREAM AND FOIE GRAS

(Makes 4 appetizers)

John Newman was arguably the busiest—and most colorful—chef of the three-day festival in 2016. Newman does not look like your typical white-tablecloth restaurateur. A man of medium height with a long drape of sandy blond hair, John arrived at the festival sporting a tie-dye shirt, Chuck Taylor high tops, and a beaver coat. "Ah, now there's a *true* represen-

Recipe courtesy of Chef John Newman, Newmans at 988

tative of the Beaver State!" I thought. Everyone loved John's eclectic attire and flamboyant attitude, both of which added to his dishes' charm.

Newman cooked Friday at the festival's kick-off party, Saturday at a winery luncheon, and put on a mouthwatering cooking demonstration on Sunday. I was extremely fortunate to taste all his creations over the three days, but this dish, which he showcased during his cooking demo, left me slack jawed. As soon as John spooned the pasta onto my plate, I sought a spot with better lighting, so I could snap a photo. Luckily, there was nobody around. His pasta was so incredibly savory, I literally licked my plate clean. There's no way I would have done that in public view. But in this quiet, empty corner, I had no shame.

At a glance, the dish looks so unassuming—just a few ingredients simply prepared—yet it's so utterly luxurious. Newman's secret is the foie gras and Oregon black truffles. If you can get your hands on these two ingredients (and remember, though they are pricey, you don't need a lot), I implore you to try this dish. Nothing transforms pasta in cream sauce into decadent bliss quite like this recipe.

INGREDIENTS

2 ounces shallots, chopped
2 cups marsala wine
6 ounces cream
1 teaspoon fresh lemon juice
Sea salt, to taste
Pepper, freshly ground, to taste
8 ounces pasta of your choice, cooked (Newman used torchio pasta—always fun)

4 ounces fresh, grade-A foie gras (foie gras in America is always of duck, and it is often sold in 2-ounce slices—so use 2 slices for this recipe)
2 tablespoons fresh flat-leaf parsley, minced
4 grams Oregon black truffles, shaved

PREPARATION

In a medium saucepan, combine shallots and marsala. Reduce to approximately 4 ounces of liquid. Add cream and reduce by half. Finish with lemon juice, salt, and pepper.

While the sauce is reducing, cook the pasta according to package directions and heat a small, dry skillet over high heat. Season the top of the foie gras with salt and pepper, then pan sear seasoned side down first. Flip after 30 seconds to 1 minute (or as soon as deep caramel crust is formed) and then sear the other side another 30 seconds or so. Remove to a warmed plate lined with paper towels to drain, then slice into ½-inch cubes.

Add cooked pasta and fresh parsley to the marsala cream sauce and toss. Season with additional salt and pepper if desired. Add shaved truffles and seared foie gras to the pasta, toss again, serve, and enjoy!

DUNGENESS CRAB AND WHITE TRUFFLE TARTLETS

(Makes 12 hors d'oeuvres)

Recipe courtesy of Karl Zenk, executive chef, Marché Restaurant Group

The OTF weekend kicked off with a boisterous Friday night happy hour at Provisions Market Hall, a popular public market and wine bar offering an enviable assortment of artisan cheeses, charcuterie, and other specialty foods, along with top quality fish and meats. But this evening there was a lot more to sample, as the staff prepared a variety of appetizers highlighting Oregon truffles. Some bites were French influenced, such as a silky truffle duck liver pâté, while others were mainstream American fare, like mac 'n' cheese and pizza garnished with freshly shaved truffle. A crowd favorite was the seared top sirloin with a choice of truffle cream or truffle demi-glace accompaniment.

For me, the stars in the market that evening were the dishes that paired Oregon white truffles with native PNW seafood. I found these flavors dazzling, and incomparably complementary, as if you couldn't taste one without the other. I didn't think anything could be more blissful than that bite of poached Coho salmon with white truffle crème fraîche (shown in the background of the photograph). Then I tried this diminutive but delightful Dungeness crab tartlet and was instantly bewitched by its sumptuously divine flavors. After that bite, I knew I was forever to be an ardent admirer and staunch advocate of Oregon truffles.

INGREDIENTS

Pastry Crust

8 ounces butter

13¼ ounces all-purpose flour

1½ teaspoons salt

3¼ ounces cold water

Truffle Crab Salad

½ pound Dungeness crab meat

1 small stalk celery, small dice

1 lemon, zested and juiced

½ clove garlic, grated on a microplane

1 fresh Oregon white truffle, grated on a microplane to taste, plus more for garnish

1 tablespoon fresh dill, chopped

1 tablespoon fresh chives, chopped

½ cup quality mayonnaise, preferably homemade

Sea salt, to taste

Pepper, freshly ground, to taste

PREPARATION

Pastry Crust

Note: if you are using barquette molds shorter than 4 inches and the pastry dough is rolled quite thin, you may be able to squeeze two-dozen hors d'oeuvres from this recipe.

Cut the butter into the flour and salt using a food processor. Add cold water and quickly bring the dough together, being careful not to overmix. Let rest in the refrigerator for an hour.

Roll out the dough on a floured board to ⅛-inch thick (or even thinner). Cut the dough to fit a barquette mold and press into the molds. Place another mold on top of the dough and bake at 350°F for 15 to 20 minutes until light golden in color.

Let the crust cool, then remove from the molds.

Truffle Crab Salad

Gently mix the crab with the celery, lemon juice and zest, garlic, truffle, and chopped herbs. Add the mayonnaise a little at a time until you like the consistency. Season with salt and pepper.

Spoon a dollop of the salad into the barquette tart shells and garnish with more freshly grated white truffle.

2

Shelton:

FROM TIDE TO TABLE

Oyster barges in the shallows of Puget Sound.

◇◇◇◇◇◇◇◇◇◇◇◇◇◇◇◇◇◇

Leaving Interstate 5 at Olympia for Highway 101 is one of my favorite driving diversions. Immediately after the fork, the scenery changes. Between the evergreen thickets of firs, spruces, cedars, and pines, you see snatches of calm, slate-blue water and gravelly beaches. The landscape smells clean and fresh, and feels like life—like anything could live here, happily and healthy.

So, it was no surprise that when I pulled into Shelton, I found a spot of aquatic landscape teeming with creatures: oysters, mussels, and clams, big and small—the type of life that seems almost primordial. It is a landscape that is soon recognizable as one that spawns animals of all sorts.

And it is here that I got my first glimpse of one such prehistoric-looking creature. With neither face nor limb, housed in a shell ridiculously inadequate for its size and vermiform body, it seems incomprehensible that we Earthlings would want to taste this creature. More incredible is that the flavor of such an alien creature is so heavenly.

DUCK, DUCK, GEODUCK

Presentation is everything. Foods we might ordinarily shun suddenly become mouthwatering if prepared and arranged in a manner that is pleasing to the eye. But even the most artistic chefs struggle with the geoduck. My word, what a hideous thing. This resident of the southern waters of Puget Sound possesses an appearance that only a mother could love (and believe me, the mother needs help, too). There really is no G-rated way to describe a geoduck: it absolutely looks like an enormous, flaccid, uncircumcised penis spilling out of a clam shell. Oy vey!

Ironically, it is the geoduck's phallic appearance that makes it such a beloved creature around the Sound. Evergreen State College, situated in the northwest corner of Olympia, adopted the geoduck as its official mascot, along with the motto *Omnia Extares*, Latin for *Let it all hang out*. And its otherworldly form has been relished lately on food TV. The mollusk has rocketed to celebrity status, shocking (and revolting) contestants on *Top Chef* and *Top Chef Masters*, *Chopped*, *Iron Chef America*, and *Dinner: Impossible*.

But the geoduck's unappetizing physiology belies its truly delectable flavor. It is a firm, meaty, succulent shellfish, particularly relished by Asian cultures. This American native creature may not be a mainstay in our popular seafood eateries, but in sushi kitchens and Chinese restaurants, geoduck is a delicacy that can fetch exorbitant prices.

I should point out that this mollusk suffers not only from an unsightly appearance, but a befuddling moniker. If you've never heard of geoduck until now, I bet you've been butchering its name as you've been reading this. It is not pronounced *gee-oh-duck*, but *gooey-duck*. And the name has nothing to do with ducks at all.

Most likely, the spelling of geoduck is the result of a poor transcription of the Nisqually word *gwe-duc*, which means "dig deep." Using their "foot," a small appendage that comes out of what most of us would incorrectly assume is the butt of the geoduck, the clam bores deep into the tidal sand. But as the geoduck descends further into the earth, its siphon, or "neck" (the phallic-looking part of the clam) needs to remain above ground,

Audrey Lamb, of Taylor Shellfish Farms, shows off an enviable geoduck.

drawing food and air from the tidal waters. The geoduck's shell might only be six inches long, but its siphon can extend well over three feet, sometimes six feet for very mature specimens. Geoducks are the largest burrowing clams in the world, and one of the longest-living animals. Because they burrow so deeply, they are quite difficult to harvest, which protects these tidal creatures; few predators can pull a two-pound clam out of four feet of tidal muck. Thus, the geoduck lives largely free from harm, for as long as 140 years. (The oldest specimen on record was 168 years old.)

◇◇◇◇◇◇◇◇◇◇◇◇◇◇◇◇◇

I was in town to visit Taylor Shellfish Farms, to see their facility and to catch my first glimpse of a live geoduck. I had known geoduck were endemic to the Pacific Northwest, but I learned they are particularly abundant in and around Puget Sound. Taylor Shellfish Farms began their operations in the Totten Inlet of Puget Sound in 1890, cultivating the native, diminutive, and increasingly endangered Olympia oyster. Since then, they've expanded their aquaculture to include a variety of oysters, mussels, clams, and geoducks. Taylor is not only the largest producer of geoduck in the region, they are the largest producer of farmed shellfish in the United States.

The shellfish are spawned in tanks, and the resultant "seed" is planted in the tidal flats around the Sound. Here, geoducks and oysters will feed for years until they grow to a marketable size. Millions of geoducks alone are cultivated by Taylor Shellfish Farms at any given time. The sheer quantities of mollusks Taylor can cultivate is testament to the fecund waters of south Puget Sound.

When I arrived at Taylor Shellfish, I met Audrey Lamb, biological project manager at Taylor. I learned a lot about aquaculture and shellfish from Lamb as we quickly toured the facility.

Audrey Lamb points to the clean, plump belly of one of Taylor Shellfish Farms' geoducks.

She took me to the geoduck tanks and explained a bit of the bivalve's anatomy. Like that of all bivalves—clams, mussels, oysters—the geoduck's shell consists of two similarly sized "valves" or plates, hinged along one edge by a flexible ligament. Unlike the smaller bivalves, the geoduck is too large to retreat into its shell. But it doesn't need to for protection from predators; deep burrowing in a mudflat is an even better defense. I asked Audrey, "So, what part of this do we actually eat?" She then showed me why Taylor Shellfish geoducks are so prized.

As with any creature—mammal, bird, or fish—there are certain physiological features to look for when determining top culinary quality. She explained the two principal parts of the geoduck—the siphon, or "neck," through which the clam feeds and breathes; and the other end, the part that protrudes out all sides of its undersized shell. This is the mantle, or "belly," and Lamb says the best geoducks have stout necks and clean, plump, bright bellies. She pulled a geoduck out of the tank and showed me. When she pointed to its mantle, I finally understood why many find this clam so appetizing. It was easy to imagine that succulent, white belly meat sliced, breaded, and panfried.

XINH YUMMY

Taylor Shellfish Farms has become a large, industrial operation along the shores of Puget Sound, employing over seven hundred workers and cultivating thousands of acres of tidelands. But they still operate a tiny seafood counter that never lost its genuine mom-and-pop feel. After my tour of the plant, Lamb and I headed to the seafood counter, as I was eager to see what they had on display, maybe even sample a half dozen of their fresh oysters. There were two steaming pots of chowder off to the side, one geoduck, the other oyster. As I was mulling over their menu, a short, stout, merry-faced lady emerged from the back. Lamb introduced me to Xinh Dwelley, a prominent chef in Shelton who runs a clam and oyster eatery owned by Taylor Shellfish Farms. Dwelley is no stranger to food journalists, I discovered, regardless of medium: she's been featured in countless local newspapers, magazines, radio programs, and even appeared alongside Mike Rowe on his TV series *Dirty Jobs*. During that episode, Taylor Shellfish staff taught Rowe how to harvest geoduck clams from the tidelands, and Xinh showed him how to clean them. Audrey said if I really wanted to learn how to cook geoduck, Xinh Dwelley was the best instructor.

Xinh was very polite but obviously quite busy that day, and she seemed focused on something else. We exchanged hellos, and I explained briefly why I was visiting from California, and that I was really intrigued with geoduck. She suddenly turned to me said, "Wait right here."

She disappeared in the back and I continued my conversation with Audrey. A few minutes later, Xinh emerged with a gorgeous dish: a geoduck ceviche with Thai influences—peanuts, chilis, garlic, lime, and julienned carrots, garnished with a fresh sprig of mint. I was speechless. We spoke for all of thirty seconds, and I know my presence was a disruption in her busy day. But before I could finish my conversation with Audrey and say, "I'll take a bowl of your geoduck chowder," Xinh emerged with something I'd expect to find in only the most *haute* of seafood establishments.

I thanked Xinh for her scrumptious, surprise meal and the warm conversation. I wanted to speak with her more about geoduck and her entertaining culinary experiences, but she had to leave to get to her restaurant. She suggested I stop by sometime, and she would introduce me to a host of various geoduck dishes. This was not to be missed.

I arrived that same night. The town of Shelton is small, quiet, working class, and charming. Dwelley's restaurant was cozy and unassuming; not the least pretentious, and there were even a couple kids running about. It felt like the kind of restaurant my mom would have, if she had a restaurant. I went back to the kitchen and said hi to Xinh, who was busy shelling and cleaning a few geoducks. As she'd done for Mike Rowe, she gave me a quick lesson on how clean these clams.

First, grab a geoduck with tongs and blanch it for six seconds, then plunge it into an ice bath. This kills the geoduck and allows the tough, wrinkly, elephant-trunk-like skin that encases the neck to be pulled off easily and cleanly. (If you stretch out the casing, you can see just how long the siphon of that geoduck is. This one looked to be close to four feet long!) Next, insert a knife between the shell and the meat and slice the muscle. Repeat for the other side. Now you will see the naked geoduck, with all its viscera. But cleaning is easy; simply grab the guts with one hand and give them a quick tug and they will pull free. Finally, cut the neck (siphon) from the belly, and rinse the pieces to remove any sand. You now have two cuts of meat, essentially. The belly is great for frying, but the neck is sweeter, although a bit crunchier; like jellyfish if you've ever had it.

After my quick lesson, I made my way to a table, passing a plastic model of a geoduck that waitstaff use to educate patrons about the anatomy of this unique bivalve. "Xinh uses the neck for sashimi, because it is firmer, and pairs well with soy and wasabi," my server explains. "She uses the belly for pan frying, because the neck would be too tough."

Then, the dishes started coming out. Xinh is Vietnamese, but she has a fondness for Thai flavors. The first dish was steamed mussels in a curry sauce. I have to say, as good as her geoduck ceviche was earlier that day, this Thai-inspired dish was phenomenal and so exquisitely balanced. I've never had a dish where such bold, complex flavors still allowed the clean, fresh flavors of mussels to shine through.

Then the geoduck arrived. First, another raw preparation. The sashimi—which is sliced entirely from the neck—was firm and chewy, with a slight crunch, but very light in flavor, with a

Xinh Dwelley's geoduck sashimi.

taste of the sea. Soy, wasabi, and pickled ginger are the standard accompaniments to sushi, though I find all three together can overpower the delicate flavors of many species of fresh fish. Not so with geoduck.

Then came the belly dish. Thick slices of panko-breaded, pan-fried meat. Other than the unique spices Dwelley used when breading the geoduck, it was a remarkably simple dish. But it was perfectly cooked. Imagine the most succulent calamari, light on the palate, though, and you are close. This is how fried fish should be. Though there are many ways to cook a clam, geoduck was made for frying. My fritters were so meaty, juicy, and tender—like great, free-range fried chicken—but exceptionally sweet. This dish would turn anyone who might be squeamish about geoduck into an ardent fan.

ODE TO AN OYSTER

There are just five oyster species cultivated in the United States, and only two of those are native. Up and down the Atlantic coast, regardless if you are slurping on PEIs, Blue Points, or Rappahannock Rivers, you are eating the same species, our native Eastern oyster. These oysters will look distinct and have unique flavors, but only because of the inimitable waters in which they live. Similarly, if you're on the West Coast shucking Hog Island Sweetwaters, Hama Hamas, or Penn Coves, you are opening all the same Japanese Pacific species. Kumamoto is another imported species grown in the United States, as well as the European Flat. But the fifth species grown in America is truly special.

Olympia oysters are the only native oyster of the West Coast. As recently as 1800, they were abundant from Alaska to Southern California. (Though there's some debate. A recent *Scientific American* article notes that Olympias were never native to California. While Olys were found in San Francisco Bay, they were introduced from northerly latitudes by enterprising oyster fishermen, but they could never get the finicky Olympias to spawn in the warmer California waters.) By the time of the Gold Rush, Olympia oyster beds were being decimated from overharvesting by pioneers and settlers. When Taylor Shellfish Farms started their farming operations in 1890, Olympia oyster populations were starting to see a decline even in the remoter tidelands of Oregon and Washington. From the onset, Taylor Shellfish's business model revolved around clean, healthy waters, to protect and cultivate this important, regionally distinct food source.

By the 1920s, pulp and paper mills were going full steam in the PNW, and the effluent discharged into the bays and estuaries were killing off the remaining Olympia oyster populations. By the 1950s, the Olympia oyster industry was on the verge of total collapse. The only thing that saved these mollusks from extinction in the PNW were a handful of oyster farmers in Puget Sound, like Taylor Shellfish Farms.

◇◇◇◇◇◇◇◇◇◇◇◇◇◇◇◇◇

One thing I read in Michael Pollan's *The Omnivore's Dilemma* has stayed fresh in my memory after all these years. Pollan profiled a chicken rancher, Joel Salatin, a man revered for the exceptional quality of his poultry and eggs. But Salatin said he doesn't think of himself as a chicken rancher, rather a grass farmer. You can't raise great chickens unless you have great pasture, Salatin reasons. So it is with oysters.

Taylor Shellfish sells mollusks of exceptional quality. But they are really in the business of pristine waters. Taylor cultivates Olympia oysters, but they aren't moneymakers. (Taylor Shellfish makes the bulk of their profits from Japanese Pacific varieties, like Shigoku, Kusshi, and Kumamoto.) Why cultivate something that isn't generating revenue? One reason is a tie to the past; Olympia oyster farming was the genesis of Taylor Shellfish Farms. But another is the challenge of attaining impeccable water quality.

Olympias are finicky, more so than other oyster species. They need a steady supply of phytoplankton (and the right kind of phytoplankton) and specific water temperatures with just the right salinity and mineral content to thrive. In this way, Olympias are the canary in the wharf. Puget Sound has what Olympias need, so if Olys aren't flourishing here, something's amiss.

Taylor has been instrumental in protecting the health of the region's waterways, because without high-quality water, there is no high-quality product. They collaborate with the Puget Sound Restoration Fund, a group dedicated to maintaining total ecosystem health by bolstering aquatic food species—oysters, abalone, and kelp, for example. Together, they establish community shellfish farms, which are developed specifically to engage the public in clean water efforts. Today, the future for Olympia oysters isn't rosy, but it is far from bleak. Thanks to efforts of the Puget Sound Restoration Fund and Taylor Shellfish, Olys are on the rebound.

Yes, Taylor sells shellfish; but where they spend the bulk of their intellectual energy is in ensuring clean, healthy ecosystems. Only in the Pacific Northwest is "big business" and "healthy environment" one and the same.

◇◇◇◇◇◇◇◇◇◇◇◇◇◇◇◇◇◇◇◇

Bill Taylor, part owner of Taylor Shellfish, says there is another important reason to cultivate Olympias, which he divulged to a journalist from *Sunset Magazine*: "Because they taste so darn good." Indeed, among oyster aficionados, Olys are often considered the best of the bivalves in the United States.

Rowan Jacobsen is considered one of America's foremost experts in oyster gastronomy and has authored two odes to these titillating mollusks. *A Geography of Oysters* is an excellent introduction to North America's oyster species and flavor as well as our nation's most revered oyster places, while *The Essential Oyster* is an indispensable reference for ostreaphiles (oyster geeks) seeking to deepen their knowledge of these shellfish. Olys are among Jacobsen's favorite, because they are special in flavor and place. In *A Geography of Oysters*, he writes:

> When an entire species of oyster is named for a single place on earth, you can expect something unique. You get it with Olys, which are no longer cultivated anywhere but the Olympia area—primarily Totten and Little Skookum inlets. This was the only spot the native oysters were able to escape the pollution and overharvesting that wiped them out elsewhere on the West Coast.
>
> Olys all share an unmistakable sweet, metallic, celery-salt flavor. Those from Totten are said to be more coppery, while those from Little Skookum are nutty and musky. All Olys are tiny—it takes 250 shucked meats to fill a pint . . . but they pack more flavor and interest than a full-sized Pacific or Eastern oyster.

I had read Jacobsen's account of Olympia oysters before my first trip to Shelton. I wanted to know what to expect, should I be lucky enough to find Olys. It was early July, and certainly not the best time to eat any oyster, Olympia or otherwise. That adage, "only eat oysters in months with an R," today has more to do with oyster biology as opposed to poor water quality and even poorer oyster storage and shipping methods. But it can still be a prudent rule to follow.

You don't want to eat an Oly in August. Summer is when oysters spawn, and all their energy is used in producing spat, or oyster larvae. This requires considerable effort, and that plump, juicy oyster meat you find in months with an R is now flac-

The perfect Puget Sound lunch—geoduck chowder with a half-dozen Olympia oysters at Taylor Shellfish Farms.

cid and shriveled. Even at their plumpest, Olympias don't have much meat to chew. Come August, Olys are spent.

Here I was, in the middle of summer, but there was no way I was going to miss an opportunity to try some of Taylor's Olympia oysters. I ordered a half dozen, which was not nearly enough. Like Jacobsen said, Olys are tiny. The shells on mine were a little larger than a fifty-cent piece, but the meats no bigger than a quarter. I'm not sure a dozen would have been enough. But if you're worried about the price don't fret. These Olys might be the best deal in America. Taylor Shellfish sells Olympia oysters for a dollar each. When it comes to oysters, there is no greater bang for the buck.

Even though July is awfully close to spawning season, I found these Olympias captivating and delicious. I didn't notice the coppery flavor that is said to be inherent in Olys, but maybe that flavor is quieted as the oyster gets closer to spawning.

I returned to Taylor Shellfish in February the following year and sampled Olympias again. Now we were talking; these oysters were exquisite. The metallic taste hit me right away. I can't say copper definitively (it had been a long time since I last put pennies in my mouth), but certainly metal of some sort. But the metallic taste wasn't overwhelming, nor did it last. The finish was light and clean, like celery and salt. Just as I had expected, and just as I had hoped.

GEODUCK RECIPES (AND AN OYSTER COCKTAIL)

I've eaten oysters prepared a variety of ways: stewed, grilled, deep-fried, pan-fried, smoked, and Rockefeller'd. When you have large, fat oysters, cooking can be the best way to eat them, as the meat is too generous for the single slurp of eating them raw. But Olympia oysters are tiny, most barely the size of a quarter. Besides, they are so rare, you will likely never encounter them unless you're around Puget Sound. Even there, they can be hard to source. For these reasons, Olys should never be cooked. I will even go so far as to say, skip the mignonette. You'll want to taste them pure, unadulterated, to really experience their unique flavor.

Geoduck, on the other hand, can and should be enjoyed many ways. I loved Xinh Dwelley's raw dishes—her simple sashimi and her ceviche were light, delicate, and immensely satisfying, while showcasing fresh geoduck flavor. But the best geoduck flavor and texture is revealed when these giant clams are breaded and fried.

Following are a few geoduck recipes that were the highlights of my many visits to Puget Sound. Regardless of the preparation you choose for your meal, whet your appetite with a stiff and briny oyster martini.

OYSTER MARTINI

(Yields 1 cocktail)

Recipe courtesy of Dan Severt, Taylor Shellfish Oyster Bar, Queen Anne

Next time you're in Seattle, do your mouth a favor and visit one of Taylor Shellfish Farms' neighborhood oyster bars. These are gastronomic jewels within the Emerald City, a place to grab a stiff cocktail or chilled brew while sampling some of the West Coast's freshest and finest oysters, clams, and geoduck. During one of my recent visits, I popped into the Queen Anne location around happy hour, hoping to taste what I thought would be the ultimate oyster and spirits pairing: an Olympia oyster martini. But I hit a snag.

Dan Severt is the affable bar manager at Taylor's Queen Anne oyster bar, and when I gave him my drink order, he shook his head. "I've tried it time and again, and the oyster flavor is lost," Dan said. "All you will taste is the alcohol." When Severt came to Taylor Restaurants, he had grand ideas to invent all sorts of oyster cocktails, with the oyster martini being the pinnacle. But he warned me, it just doesn't work.

I was dejected, but I had to try the martini anyway. I also told Dan I'd like to photograph the cocktail, in case I wanted to use it for this book. I had a vivid image in my mind of how the martini could be prepared so that the oysters were highlighted. "Can you skewer the oysters with a toothpick—like you would olives—and lay that across the rim of the glass?"

"Absolutely not," Dan replied. "That goes against everything we stand for at Taylor Shellfish." He continued, "Look, we serve the best, freshest oysters . . . these things are alive and we want them to stay that way right up until they hit your tongue. I am not going to stab one for a photograph."

I appreciated Severt's candor and Taylor's food philosophy, even though it meant I couldn't get the photo I wanted for the book. Dan's polite refusal to accommodate my request underscores Taylor Shellfish Farms' "no compromise" ethic when it comes to freshness and flavor. And we are all damn lucky for that.

Alas, Dan was right. The martini was fabulous, but I couldn't discern oyster flavor—even with Dan's recipe alterations. He used vodka instead of gin; only ¼ ounce of vermouth instead of the more typical ½ ounce; and he used three oysters even though I thought one would be plenty. All of Dan's modifications were intended to lift as much oyster flavor through the cocktail as possible. It was all for naught.

But sometimes mistakes lead to blissful discoveries. Kevin— a refreshingly opinionated and brusque waiter who prefers to go by Stump—suggested I deconstruct the martini. "Don't complicate it. Just enjoy the martini and eat the oysters on the side," he suggested. "It's a great pairing." But I didn't want to fish out my oysters from the bottom of my glass, so I ordered three fresh ones. The instructions were simple: Slurp the oyster, give it a good chew, then take sip of the martini. "SuperSonics, Stump you're right!" The flavors were a perfect complement.

When my glass was drained, the real treat still lay at the bottom. Why the oyster flavor failed to permeate the martini, I'll never know. But the martini certainly infused those plump oysters, and when I bit down on those drunken bivalves, an incomparably delicious mix of sea and spirit flavor flooded my mouth. That evening, I discovered that a simple dunking into a vodka martini proved to be a better oyster condiment than any cocktail sauce or mignonette.

INGREDIENTS

6 small Taylor Shellfish oysters (Olympia, Shigoku, or Kumamoto are fine choices)
3 ounces top shelf vodka (Severt suggested Tito's. It was an excellent recommendation)
¼ ounce dry vermouth (Severt chose Dolin Vermouth de Chambéry)

PREPARATION

Begin by shucking the oysters. Place three on the half shell on a small plate. Pour the other three—including the oyster liquor—into a chilled martini glass.

Measure the vodka and vermouth into a cocktail shaker then fill with ice. Stir until well chilled. Strain the spirits into the martini glass with the oysters.

Now, take a good sip or two from the glass, and slurp one of the oysters on your plate. Repeat until the 3 plated oysters and spirits have been consumed. What is left—three drunken oysters in the bottom of a martini glass—will be the heavenly finish to a marvelous happy hour cocktail and appetizer.

XINH'S GEODUCK CEVICHE

(Makes 2 servings)

Recipe courtesy of Xinh Dwelley, formerly of Xinh's Clam and Oyster House

This is the amazing dish Xinh Dwelley prepared for me within minutes of our introduction. She is one of the most gracious and talented cooks I've ever met, with no equal when it comes to geoduck.

When you're as familiar with geoducks as Xinh is, you will

be able to prepare this ceviche in about fifteen minutes. But it won't take much longer for the novice; skinning and cleaning these clams isn't nearly as intensive as it is for other fish.

Once, in Seattle, I had a fabulous geoduck crudo, and Dwelley's simple geoduck sashimi is delightful. But I love this raw geoduck dish best because of the creative Thai spin. Limes, sesame, peanuts, chilis, garlic, fish sauce—ingredients that form the foundational flavors of pad thai work equally well with raw geoduck. Maybe even better.

INGREDIENTS

1 live Taylor Shellfish geoduck, about 1 pound (We'll only use the siphon or "neck" meat for this recipe—save the belly for the Geoduck Fritters on page 73), thinly sliced

2 medium limes, juiced

1 celery stalk, thinly sliced

1 small carrot, julienned

1 medium cucumber, thinly sliced lengthwise, skin on

¼ cup onion, chopped

2 tablespoons sesame seeds

1 clove of garlic, minced

2 red chili peppers, chopped

1 tablespoon fish sauce

1 tablespoon brown sugar

2 sprigs of mint, chiffonade cut, plus extra for garnish

⅓ cup roasted peanuts, chopped

PREPARATION

Preparing geoduck might seem daunting to the novice cook; but it is surprisingly easy. There are two ways to prep a geoduck before cooking: clean the clam first then blanch the meat, or blanch the live clam—shell and all—and clean afterward. The fastidious and squeamish will certainly prefer the latter method, and if we weren't going to use the belly meat for the next recipe, boiling the live geoduck whole would suffice. But this dish is best using only the siphon or "neck," and the next recipe for Geoduck Fritters is best using the mantle or "belly." The belly meat used for the fritters will be fried very quickly, and we don't want to blanch it and then fry it, as the meat will overcook. For this recipe and the next, it is best to shuck and clean the geoduck first. Here's how.

Begin by filling a small stock pot or large sauce pan (something big enough to hold the geoduck) half full with water and bring to a boil. Insert a sharp knife between the shell and the clam and cut the shell free. Repeat on the other side. You will now be able to see the entire naked clam with its viscera. Simply grab the viscera and pull it away from the body; it will separate quite easily. Trim away any remaining innards until the belly looks clean and neat.

The geoduck's siphon is encased in a tough membrane that should be removed before eating. This is why we blanch geoduck: to facilitate removal of the neck casing much like we would blanch a tomato to ease removal of its skin. Pick up the clam from its belly and dunk the neck into the boiling water, being careful to keep the belly meat above the water line so it doesn't cook. Blanch the neck for no more than 10 seconds, and then immediately submerge the geoduck into a bowl of ice water to halt cooking. Once cooled, you can strip that tough membrane from the siphon cleanly and easily, much like removing a latex glove from your hand. Cut off the very tip of the siphon, as this can be tough and chewy as well, then thinly slice the neck meat (reserving the belly for the next recipe). Put the sliced geoduck into a mixing bowl and add the juice of one lime and toss. Marinate for 30 minutes.

While the geoduck is marinating, combine the celery, carrot, cucumber, onion, and sesame seeds in another mixing bowl. In a separate, smaller bowl, whisk together the juice of the other lime, the garlic, red chili peppers, fish sauce, and brown sugar. Pour this sauce into the bowl with the veggies.

Now add the sliced mint and geoduck meat to the veggie bowl and gently toss again. Spoon the ceviche onto each geoduck shell and serve on small plates garnished with mint and chopped peanuts.

GEODUCK FRITTERS WITH RÉMOULADE

(Makes 8–10 fritters)

Recipe courtesy of executive chef Wesley Hood, AQUA by El Gaucho

I was introduced to geoduck fritters at Xinh Dwelley's restaurant in Shelton. Xinh's talent with this giant clam might be unrivaled, and I was fortunate to have dined in her eatery before she retired. When I learned her Clam and Oyster House was shuttered, I fretted her fabulous fritters were never going to be tasted again. It was certainly a sad time for epicureans in the PNW.

I asked if I could include her recipe in this book. Xinh politely declined, but only because—lucky for us—she is saving that recipe for her own cookbook. (And when it comes out, treat yourself and buy a copy; her geoduck fritters and curried mussels are pure gastronomic gold.)

In the meantime, I found chef Wesley Hood, and if Dwelley can be considered the queen of the geoduck, then Hood is king. Hood is the executive chef at AQUA by El Gaucho, a Seattle waterfront seafood house that Gayot ranked as one of the ten best in Seattle in 2016. Hood's geoduck fritters are a crowd favorite at AQUA, and, luckily for any foodie not in the Seattle area, he shows how easy they are to make in an instructional YouTube video—including how to properly shuck and clean a geoduck. (Check out El Gaucho's YouTube channel for this and other fantastic recipe tutorials.) Just watching Hood's video reignited my passion for this simple yet utterly delightful seafood appetizer.

Here is Wes Hood's recipe for geoduck fritters:

INGREDIENTS

Rémoulade

1 egg yolk
3 tablespoons Dijon mustard
2 tablespoons grain mustard

2 cups canola oil
½ cup extra virgin olive oil
1 lemon, juiced

½ teaspoon Kosher salt
4 tablespoons shallots, minced
3 tablespoons capers
2 tablespoons cornichons or
    dill pickles, minced

2 tablespoons chives, minced
1 tablespoon garlic, minced
1 tablespoon Tabasco hot
    sauce

Geoduck

2–3 cups flour
4 eggs
3 cups panko bread crumbs
Peanut, grapeseed, avocado, or
    any neutral-flavored cooking
    oil suitable for deep frying

Geoduck "belly" meat (see
    previous recipe, Xinh's Geo-
    duck Ceviche)
Generous pinch each of sea
    salt and pepper
2 tablespoons chives, minced
1 lemon, cut into wedges

PREPARATION

Rémoulade

In a mixing bowl, whisk the egg yolk and the two mustards until thoroughly combined and the mixture begins to pale in color. Slowly add the oils while whisking to emulsify. Add the lemon juice and continue to whisk until the sauce has the viscosity of a mayonnaise. (You can add a little water if the sauce is too thick.)

Now add the salt, shallots, capers, cornichons, chives, garlic, and hot sauce into the bowl and whisk together until combined.

Geoduck

Begin by setting up your breading stations. Place the flour in one bowl and then beat the eggs with a fork in another bowl. Pour the bread crumbs into a third bowl.

Pour cooking oil into a large skillet to a depth of about ¼ inch. Heat the oil to 360°F over medium heat.

While the oil is heating, slice the geoduck belly into ⅛-inch thick strips. With one hand (your "dry" hand), dip a geoduck piece into the flour. Shake off the excess flour and then drop the strip into the egg wash. With the other hand (your "wet" hand), remove the clam from the eggs and dip it into the bread crumbs. Using your "dry" hand, pack the panko onto the meat. Repeat this process until all the geoduck pieces are breaded.

Gently drop the geoduck into the hot oil and fry quickly—about 15 seconds, or until breading begins to turn golden brown. Quickly remove the pieces from the oil and drain on a paper-towel-lined mixing bowl. Season the geoduck fritters with a pinch of salt and pepper, some chives, and a squirt of lemon juice from a wedge or two.

Divide the fritters onto two small plates and garnish with additional minced chives and lemon wedges. Spoon the rémoulade into two ramekins and serve.

GEODUCK DEEP-DISH PIE

(Makes 8 servings)

I met Kate McDermott at her quaint house in Port Angeles, which doubles as her baking studio, a place she has named Pie Cottage. McDermott is an acclaimed pie cook in the PNW, some say the best in the region, if not one of the best makers of pie *ever*. Her pies have been featured in *USA Today*, the *New York Times*, the *Boston Globe*, *Saveur*, and on NPR. She invited

Recipe courtesy of Kate McDermott, Art of the Pie

me to Pie Cottage and revealed her secrets to the lightest, flakiest, tastiest crust I've ever had.

Kate worked for Taylor Shellfish for quite a few years, and it was there she became fond of geoduck and merged her newfound reverence for this bivalve with her passion for pie. Folks who aren't as well versed in various seafood dishes often look askance at Kate when she speaks lovingly of her geoduck pie. "Do you like pot pie?" Kate asks. Of course, everyone does. "And do you like clam chowder? Well, geoduck is just a big clam. And geoduck pie is clam chowder in a pastry crust." Once we begin to think of geoduck in that way, a whole world of potential recipes opens for us.

This is the recipe Kate created for Taylor Shellfish Farms, and she says it is her favorite savory pie. She made this dish for me at her Pie Cottage in Port Angeles, and I have to say it is my favorite savory pie as well. She included it in her James

Beard nominated memoir *Art of the Pie: A Practical Guide to Homemade Crusts, Fillings, and Life*, but she very graciously allowed me to reprint it here.

Kate secured a beautiful geoduck for our lunch from Taylor Shellfish. I held it in my hands, the first geoduck I had ever cradled. "Hold the siphon up to your ear," Kate said. "Listen. You can hear the air whooshing in." It was a stark awakening for me. No matter how alien a creature may look, it becomes instantly relatable once we hear it breathe.

Of course, Kate already knew that. She is one of the kindest people I have ever met, a lover of all things living. When it came time to prepare the pie filling, Kate brought a stock pot of water to a boil, lit a candle, and said a few thoughtful, respectful words to our geoduck. We then executed the first step in Kate's recipe in solemn silence.

INGREDIENTS

Pie Dough

2½ cups King Arthur unbleached white flour (red bag), chilled in freezer

8 tablespoons of leaf lard, cut into various small pieces from pea to walnut size

8 tablespoons of Irish butter, cut into various small pieces from pea to walnut size

½ teaspoon kosher salt

8–10 tablespoons of ice water (more if needed)

Filling

1 geoduck, about 1½–2½ pounds
1 onion, chopped
5 red potatoes, diced
4 cloves garlic, chopped fine
2 stalks celery, chopped

1 handful of Italian flat-leaf parsley, chopped
3 tablespoons good quality olive oil
8 strips of bacon
½ teaspoon sage
½ teaspoon rosemary
1 teaspoon thyme
1–2 tablespoons Mama Lil's Peppers (These are a Pacific
Northwest treasure: pickled Hungarian goathorn peppers
packed in oil. Any pickled Hungarian pepper will suffice,
but I'm convinced Mama Lil's is the best for this recipe. If
for nothing else, buy a jar for the whimsical label and corny
slogan: "The *Peppatunities* are endless!")
Salt and pepper to taste
Oregon black truffle, a few shavings

Pie Assembly

1 egg yolk   2 teaspoons water

PREPARATION

Pie Dough

Place flour, lard, butter, and salt into a large bowl. Using your
fingers, blend together until the mixture is incompletely mixed
and its parts range in size from cracker crumb, to pea, to
almond. Sprinkle ice-cold water over the mixture, then gently stir with a fork until dough starts to feel sluggish. Gather
the dough together with your hands and form into a big ball.
Halve the dough, then form into 2 chubby disks, each about
5 inches in diameter. Wrap the disks separately in plastic wrap
and refrigerate for 1 hour.

Unwrap a dough disk, then transfer to a well-floured surface. Whack it with a rolling pin several times; turn it over and

repeat. Roll out the dough to form an 11- to 12-inch circle, then transfer it to a 9- or 10-inch deep-dish pie pan. If dough tears and needs mending, dab a little water where it requires patching and "glue" on a piece of dough. Repeat for the other dough disk once the filling has been added into the pie shell. (This will be your top crust.)

Filling

Bring a large pot of water to boil. With tongs, quickly submerge the entire geoduck, shell and all, in the boiling water. After 10 seconds remove the geoduck with tongs.

Run a sharp knife along the inside of each shell to cut away the geoduck meat. Once shelled, make an additional cut along the middle of the body and remove and discard the viscera. Remove the siphon casing on the long neck of the geoduck, and chop off the dark, rubbery tip. Rinse the body and siphon meat well in very cold water; the meat should now resemble raw chicken. Dice the mantle and siphon meat into bite-sized pieces, much as you would for chicken stir fry or stew, then set aside.

Sauté the onions, potatoes, garlic, celery, and parsley in olive oil over medium low heat. In another pan, cook the bacon over medium heat until most of the fat has been rendered, but the bacon is still soft. Remove the bacon and drain on paper towels. Then chop into 1-inch pieces and add to the other skillet with the onions and potatoes and such. Add the herbs, geoduck, and Hungarian peppers, and cook slowly a few more minutes. Add salt and pepper to taste, then finish with freshly shaved Oregon black truffle. Set the filling aside to cool.

Pie Assembly

Preheat oven to 425°F. Pour the cooled filling into the crust-lined pie pan. Roll out the top crust and place over the filling. Crimp the edges and cut a few vents on top of the pie. Using a fork, beat the egg yolk and water together in small bowl and brush over the top of the pie. Place the assembled pie on the center rack of the oven and bake for 20 minutes. Turn oven down to 375°F and bake for an additional 30 to 35 minutes until you see some steam coming out of the vents and the top of the pie is golden.

Let the pie cool for at least 10 minutes (the filling will remain hot for quite some time). Slice into eight equal pieces and serve.

3

Olympia:
IT'S THE WATER

Budd Inlet—the southernmost arm of Puget Sound, and the doorstep to Olympia.

◇◇◇◇◇◇◇◇◇◇◇◇◇◇◇◇◇◇

After my visit with the folks at Taylor Shellfish, I left Shelton and decided to motor around the Sound and up to Seattle. First, a pit stop in Olympia. I wanted to explore the capital city a bit and walk along Budd Inlet, the southernmost tip of Puget Sound, to gain a better sense of the landscape where Olympia oysters derived their name. Oh, and it was time for coffee.

My caffeine of choice is an espresso macchiato, and there is a coffee roaster in town that received glowing Yelp reviews and was a pioneer in the artisan coffee craze in the Pacific Northwest. I walked into Batdorf & Bronson's espresso bar, ordered my coffee, and chatted with the barista. While she was extracting the double ristretto shots for my drink, I told her why I was visiting the region, which led to the subject of water. "The key to great coffee is great water," she said, a maxim I've heard a few times from baristas and brewers alike. "If you're interested in native foods with unique flavor, you should check out the public well downtown."

Water? I hadn't thought of water in that way before, as a *food*, native or otherwise, with *flavor*. As I thought more about it, water can certainly have a unique taste (or an utter lack of it). And water is arguably the only truly local sustenance Americans regularly consume, regardless of season or location. The freshwater lakes, reservoirs, rivers, and wells that quench our communities lie no further than a hundred miles from our metro regions.

"Will do," I said. "Thanks for the tip!" It was then I learned, as I finished my coffee, that Olympia is famous for a few things: Washington state capital, the brief home to grunge rockers Kurt Cobain and Courtney Love, and artesian wells.

◇◇◇◇◇◇◇◇◇◇◇◇◇◇◇◇◇

I drove down Fourth Avenue, turned right on Jefferson, parked my rental, and walked a few yards into Artesian Commons. It's an asphalt parking lot really, but the northern half had recently shut out cars in favor of pedestrians. A few tables with umbrellas sprinkled about occupied what previously had been parking spaces, and many urban street youths were hanging around, chatting, skateboarding, and just chilling on their BMX bikes. And there in the middle of it all was a simple brass pipe, bent at ninetey degrees, recently encased and adorned by a pair of large concrete bollards clad in a fanciful, marine-motif mosaic.

I paused a while and stared at that pipe, likely with conspicuous incredulity. I admit, I didn't know what to expect, exactly, when the barista suggested I "check out the public well," but that brass pipe smacked of irony; for me anyway. It was July 2015, and at the time much of California was in what national government climatologists label a full-fledged D4—Exceptional Drought condition, the most parched of the US Drought Monitor classifications. I could walk on the lakebed of Folsom Reservoir (which supplies my drinking water back home) for a half mile before reaching the retreating lake edge. Our dwindling water supply left my municipality little choice but to institute residential water rationing. Yards could only be watered on certain days (and only at certain times). If there was noticeable runoff, the city came by and issued a warning. Next time, there would be fines. My neighbors ripped up their lawns and laid rock. And good for them. Water was becoming alarmingly scarce throughout California. For the state's entire seven-hundred-mile stretch, the hydrological story was the same. Field after field, in county after county, desertification seemed not only possible in the Golden State, but imminent.

Yet, just a few hundred miles north of my arid home, I was ogling a spigot spewing 10 gallons of water every minute down a storm drain; 600 gallons an hour, 14,400 gallons a day. Since those early town settlers tapped this well at the turn of the twentieth century, that's a quantity of water capable of filling a backyard swimming pool every day for over a hundred years—without any sign of let up.

Then I realized something even more astounding. This isn't any ol' tap water. This is pure, unfiltered mineral water; artesian mineral water at that! Water that is naturally clean and clear with refreshing flavor because of unhurried percolation through mineral rich stone and sand, unadulterated by humans in any way; the sort of water that is esteemed among the clientele of high-end restaurants and five-star resorts. (I've been to one restaurant that employed a water sommelier, whose menu listed almost a dozen different still and sparkling mineral waters—the most expensive from artesian aquifers.) And in this parking lot I find such special water gushing from a spout for anyone to drink—completely free.

I pulled out my camera so I could share this sight with friends and family back home. Within a few shutter clicks one of the plaza "regulars"—a young man, quite dirty, but good looking and a good life ahead of him if he would make some better choices—asked what I was doing. I explained the situation in California. I told him about our crops failing, and how Californians were asked to shower, launder, and flush less, to conserve what seemed, at the time, a finite resource.

He looked at me and blurted, "That's some crazy shit," then dropped to his knees, turned his face toward the tremendous spigot flow, and drank heartily. He spit out the last mouthful, stood up, pointed to the spout, and said, "This shit's been pouring out of the ground since, like, forever." And he was probably right. At least for the last twelve thousand years, anyway.

A WELLSPRING OF SPRINGS AND WELLS

I first witnessed Olympia's famed water that summer, but I had heard about it four decades earlier. My dad was the first to tell me about the special waters of artesian springs. He pulled out a white-and-gold can from the refrigerator and pointed to the label, which had a big horseshoe and a slogan that read "It's the Water." Then he put the can back in the fridge and said, "And that's why your mom likes Olympia beer so much."

Since then, I hadn't given much thought to springs or wells, artesian or otherwise, until that summer day in the south Sound. I was fascinated with what I had witnessed, but my dad's well-intentioned lesson didn't teach me much. (Nor did Olympia Brewing Company's promotions. While they made great fanfare over their use of artesian water, they never explained to the public what it was, preferring to claim it was special water controlled by a population of mythical "Artesians.") I kept asking myself, What *is* an artesian well, anyway? Or an artesian spring, for that matter?

After sifting through the strata of articles and papers on the subject, I learned the hydrogeological differences are very clear. A spring is just a natural outpouring of underground water up to the ground's surface; water flowing from the earth, in other words. When you dig or bore a hole to access that underground water, that is a well.

Many communities get drinking water from rivers, lakes, or reservoirs, but much of the Earth's fresh water is stored as groundwater; rainfall or snowmelt that, over time, has seeped into the soil and collects in an aquifer. I used to think of aquifers as being vast, trapped pools of freshwater—like shallow lakes, only underground. But that is not correct. An aquifer, in the simplest sense, is a highly permeable layer of earthen substrata—sand, gravel, or even porous rock, like sandstone—that is saturated. Aquifers can be found at various depths, and if the aquifer is very close to the ground's surface, we might see it discharge in the form of a spring. Similarly, we might dig (or drill) just a few feet into the ground and hit an aquifer, creating a well. We can then lower a bucket and bring the groundwater to the surface, or if higher volumes are needed, we can pump it out.

The principal difference between typical wells and artesian wells is pressure; positive hydrostatic pressure, to be exact. Think of the old-timey country well you may have witnessed or seen illustrated in your childhood storybooks. It's a deep silo of stacked stone, with a cute little gabled roof over the opening to keep leaves or other random debris from falling in. You turn a wooden crank to lower a bucket on a rope, and when the bucket hits the water way down below and fills, you crank it back up and have a gallon or two of water. This type of well isn't under much pressure; if it were, you wouldn't need to lower a bucket to bring up water.

Sometimes, an aquifer is contained below an impermeable layer of rock. The rainwater seeps through the soil as normal, but then percolates along faults and fractures, eventually collecting deep underground. As the aquifer continues to fill (or "charge," as hydrogeologists say) and the layers of rock above shift with the Earth's crust, high pressures can develop inside the aquifer. Aquifers that have a higher pressure than the atmosphere are known as artesian aquifers (after the former French province Artois, where Carthusian monks began drilling into such aquifers in the twelfth century). Puncture that layer of impermeable rock above the aquifer, and water will flow prodigiously to the surface. Congratulations! You have just created an artesian well.

If you still find the distinction of artesian water a bit muddy, let me quote a fabulous analogy from the USGS's website. I discovered this on a Q&A page designed to educate children about geology and water science (but the analogy was equally effective for this middle-aged adult). "Imagine a very wet sponge contained in a closed plastic bag. Put a straw through the bag into the sponge, hold the bag tightly around the straw, and SQUEEZE—that would be artesian water squirting you in the face." (Who knew hydrogeologists were such pranksters?)

Artesian water is abundant throughout Olympia thanks to the Cordilleran ice sheet that blanketed the Pacific Northwest during the Ice Age (our last glacial period). This massive continental glacier covered all of British Columbia, the Alaska Peninsula and panhandle, western Montana, and the Idaho panhandle. The Puget Lobe of the Cordilleran ice sheet encased the entire Puget Sound, smothering the landscape of present day Seattle, Tacoma, and Olympia. Twelve thousand years ago, when the ice sheets began melting and retreating, fresh water seeped into the ground. As the thawing hastened, rivulets formed, carrying and depositing sand around the Sound. Those rivulets that increased in water volume became streams, and then rivers, and as those rivers increased in size, new meanders were carved, and more sand was deposited here and there. Eventually, over thousands of years, many of these sand fields were covered with earth and other minerals, which eventually hardened into rock, trapping vast amounts of water deep underground. And as the ground shifted above, pressure developed below, creating artesian aquifers.

These specific geological processes mean artesian water is ancient water, quite rare, and impeccably clean. As every drop trickles deeper into the earth at a glacial pace—along a tiny fissure in stone, through the microscopic pores of a sand bed—impurities are stripped. The result is some of the purest water on earth. The well I was ogling in Artesian Commons was drilled sometime between 1895 and 1915, according to local historians. But the water flowing from that well has been determined to be over three thousand years old. Ten gallons each minute of three-thousand-year-old water spouting from a pipe in the middle of a public plaza. That is some fantastically historic, fantastically special water.

WATER WARS

I had just put my camera away when a Subaru pulled into the parking lot and stopped along the edge of the plaza. The driver opened the hatch of her wagon and removed an assortment of large containers—mostly one-gallon plastic jugs and big jars that once contained sliced kimchi. One by one, gallon by gallon, the lady filled her containers with artesian water then placed them back in her wagon—a process that, because of the well's exceptional flow rate, kept her hustling.

Curious, I asked her, "Why take the time to drive to this well and fill a dozen jugs?"

"For health reasons, mainly," she answered. "And because it's an Olympian tradition." She told me hundreds like her do the same each day: drive to the center of town to load up on this superior, free water. It wasn't that Olympia tap water was particularly expensive at the time (though our prevailing wisdom reckons *free* is better than any tariff, regardless of the good or service). Rather, it was her conviction that this ancient artesian water is far better for the human body than the well water currently being pumped to folk's homes. She also said she felt it was her responsibility—as well as every Olympian's—to continue the community tradition of gathering around the town well to quench one's thirst for hydration and social interaction. (Imagine your office watercooler, only on a much grander scale.) I must have looked puzzled, because she clarified, "Until recently, we were in danger of losing this special resource."

Citizens of Olympia today—as early settlers did over one hundred years prior—travel to the center of town to drink the ancient, pure mineral water from this famed artesian well.

Southern Puget Sound was booming at the close of the nineteenth century; Washington had just been granted statehood and Olympia was a hub of maritime commerce. As the town prospered, cultural amenities and public infrastructure followed. A new opera house was built and then a stately hotel to house visiting legislators. A streetcar line was added, gas lamps lit the sidewalks and roadways, and a public water system was constructed. But entrepreneurs found the fees for this new public water a constraint to profits. In 1895, word spread that Talcott Jewelers successfully drilled an artesian well. Other business owners followed suit and drove their own wells. Over the next two decades, almost a hundred wells were bored throughout downtown, and Olympia's artesian legacy was born.

As the region grew, more water was needed. A vast wellfield (not artesian) was constructed about five miles east of Olympia. Downtown evolved and businesses changed hands; old buildings were razed and new ones erected, and the artesian wells that once fed these properties were destroyed, paved over, or capped. By the 1990s, only a few wells remained; and only one—that brass spout bent at ninety-degrees in the middle of a downtown parking lot—was readily accessible by all comers.

Then a local psychologist had a conversation with Dick Batdorf, the cofounder of Batdorf & Bronson (that coffee shop I visited on my way to the well). He became acutely interested in preserving access to the town's artesian water after Batdorf told him, "You know, the key to great coffee is great water." (I was happy to hear Batdorf's employees are still espousing his philosophy decades later.) The city council was called in, public meetings were held, and unsolicited donations flowed. It became clear many Olympians were keen on protecting those remaining wells and preserving Olympia's artesian legacy. But this renewed interest in the town's old water ignited a battle between private businesses, public citizens, and government agencies.

In the mid-1990s, the county Department of Health ordered business owners to cap those old wells unless they could prove purity and "confinedness" (in other words, that no broken joints or cracks in the well could allow water other than the artesian source to enter). Even once confinedness and purity could be proven, frequent testing would still be necessary, to ensure the wells continued to meet health department standards. But that downtown well to which for so many years, so many of the public would drive to fill their jugs and say hi to their fellow citizens, was smack in the middle of a privately owned parking lot. And the property owners had no interest in meeting the Department of Health's demands.

Thankfully, a band of eager Olympians came to the rescue. The Friends of Artesians, whose mission was "to preserve and protect Olympia's heritage of publicly accessible artesian wells, and to promote good stewardship of these extraordinary gifts of nature," agreed to pay for regular testing and find solutions to meet all the regulatory requirements, just to keep the water flowing from that well. But their long-term goal was more ambitious: to persuade the municipality to take ownership so that public access would be guaranteed and to create an inviting urban plaza on that parking lot to celebrate Olympia's artesian legacy. The city began negotiations with the parking lot owner, but those negotiations broke down. Other sites were considered for a public well, then those sites were rejected. Twelve years later, the Friends of Artesians had spent over $20,000 on research, testing, and maintenance on that downtown parking lot well. But the Great Recession hit, talks of municipal ownership halted, and the Friends—with the fate of the well uncertain—disbanded.

Yet public demand for free access to artesian water was as strong as ever! In 2009, the *Olympian* ran a front-page story featuring the well, reporting that over a five-day survey, an average of 283 people drank from the well each day. A new coalition emerged, calling themselves H2Olympia, and adopted the slogan—It's STILL the Water. (Hey Dad, you were right! That beer *is* special!) Finally, after a twenty-year clash, there was cause for jubilation. The City of Olympia purchased the lot, kept the well open to the public 24/7, and continued the testing required by the Department of Health. After the addition of brick pavers, tables, umbrellas, raised planters, and those concrete bollards adorned with the marine-motif mosaic, Olympia had its first-ever downtown park, replete with an iconic drinking fountain; one that emits exceptional, highly coveted water.

SPAR-TESIAN

I was eager to learn more about Olympia's artesian water, so I contacted Meliss Maxfield, who has a master's degree in public health and is the program and planning supervisor with the city's public works department. Maxfield is the point person for all issues of artesian water quality, and we chatted about purity. I was curious, because when I drank the water from the downtown well that day, it tasted surprisingly clean but with a distinct metallic flavor. I couldn't quite put my tongue on it; it wasn't copper, but something quite similar. Maybe it was leached from that old one-hundred-year-old pipe, or maybe from minerals in the well, or maybe from both.

"Manganese," Maxfield answered immediately. The city tests the well water for dozens of potentially harmful contaminants, like lead and copper and arsenic and mercury and cyanide, as well as for volatile organic compounds. Many of the contaminants the municipality tests for are completely absent, and those that are detected are present in micro-quantities; far lower than the thresholds that would trigger Department of Health concerns. This is proof of the artesian water's purity. However, manganese is high in that well.

"It's nothing to be alarmed over," Maxfield reassured. "Manganese is what we call a secondary contaminant. If you are concerned about aesthetics—because manganese will eventually stain sinks and toilets and bathtubs—then you should use tap water in your home. But for drinking water, there are no health risks associated with this level of manganese in the water." Maxfield explained minerals are not equally dispersed across an aquifer. If the presence of a certain mineral is noticeably high in one well, it doesn't mean it will be the same level in another well. "It means that, when those early settlers drove that well downtown, they struck a rock or sand bed high in manganese, that's all." At the very least, the manganese gave this mineral water a distinct place-based flavor, special to downtown Olympia.

Maxfield then pointed me to the city's website, which publishes their yearly test results for the artesian well, so anyone can look up and then compare the prevalence of some two dozen minerals, salts, and metals found in the artesian water with any other source of water. (And in true Pacific Northwest spirit, the city also posts water quality results specifically for home brewers.)

◇◇◇◇◇◇◇◇◇◇◇◇◇◇◇◇◇◇

If the high manganese content dissuades you (or you're just not a fan of the taste of that particular mineral), walk three and a half blocks down Fourth Avenue to Spar Café. The Spar is one of Olympia's oldest haunts; a place where longshoremen and loggers could cash their paychecks and then promptly spend the money right back as they gambled and drank and smoked and ate. Today, the Spar is a favorite among students and legislators, and it is the only business left in downtown Olympia that still serves the public artesian water. (Though by the time you read this, the Well 80 Brewhouse will be open and serving an assortment of craft beers made with artesian water from its own well). As soon as you open the door and step into the historic building's vestibule, you will see a porcelain drinking fountain;

a chance to taste water from a different artesian well (but likely from the same aquifer, according to Maxfield). But the real artesian treats await at the bar.

Spar's website reads: "Want to try a beer made with 3,330-year-old artesian well water (give or take 50 years)? Then you've come to the right place. Our beer is brewed onsite, and the water comes from the artesian well bubbling away in the basement!" *Heck yeah* I wanted to try that beer! But I really wanted to taste the gamut of artesian beverages.

All water that flows from the taps of Spar Café is from their artesian well. That means cocktails, soups and broths, coffee— every drink and every dish they serve that needs water as an ingredient is made with artesian water. To sate my curiosity, I ordered four drinks: an India Pale Ale, a double espresso, a pot of green tea, and a glass of chilled artesian water, neat. The manganese taste I perceived from the public well was completely absent in my glass of Spar water; just clean, refreshing flavor. The tea was sublime; the way a good loose-leaf green tea should taste when made with good water heated to the perfect temperature. To be honest, the coffee and beer had too many other variables for me to say, definitively, that the artesian water helped make a superlative beverage. But you will find credence in my declaration that both were quite delicious.

I downed the last drop of my four-beverage afternoon break, thanked the server for obliging my unusual menu requests, and asked for the check. As I stood up to leave, another customer sat down at the bar two stools away from me. The last thing I heard before I exited the café was his order: "I'd like to try that beer made with the artesian water."

I smiled, and as I walked back to my rental car still parked on Jefferson Street, I pulled up Spar Café's website once more on my phone. "According to one hydrogeologist, the water is from an aquifer called the Tumwater Sand of the Holocene Epoch, a deposit of the Deschutes River (in Wa., not Ore.). The sand was

A glass of water, a cup of tea, a shot of coffee, and a pint of beer; the full menu of artesian beverages served at Spar Café.

deposited as the Deschutes re-established its channel after the last glacier withdrew from the Puget Sound, about 12,000 years ago—all of which makes for one historic pint of beer."

And I was lucky enough to drink one.

4

Port Angeles:

LOBSTER OF THE PACIFIC

Dungeness crab technicolor on display in Port Angeles.

◇◇◇◇◇◇◇◇◇◇◇◇◇◇◇◇◇◇

M y daughter was excited when I told her we were going on a family vacation to Port Angeles. It surprised me because few people outside of western Washington are familiar with the Olympic Peninsula, myself included. But then she rattled off names of tiny communities like La Push and Forks, locales only a resident of the region would know—or else, an avid reader of

Stephenie Meyer's *Twilight* series. I told my daughter Port Angeles excites me, too. But not because I wanted to hunt vampires. I was hankering flesh of a different sort . . . the sweet meat of Dungeness crab.

Port Angeles is a unique piece of geography, squeezed between the forested faces of the Olympic Mountains and the Strait of Juan de Fuca. It is the most northwestern incorporated community in the contiguous United States and lies on the northernmost point of US 101, an interstate highway that runs nearly the entire length of the continental West Coast. On a clear day, you can look out from downtown Port Angeles and see Victoria, British Columbia, and if the mood strikes, hop aboard the M/V *Coho*, which will ferry you across the Strait and into Canada. To the east of Port Angeles is Dungeness Spit, an almost seven-mile-long natural sand spit (the longest in the United States) enclosing Dungeness Bay. It is here that the Olympic Peninsula's most prized delicacy got its name. Maryland has blue crab, Maine has lobster, and Alaska has king crab. But up and down the West Coast, and especially along the northern shores of Washington, Dungeness crab is king.

Dungeness crab are not only the tastiest of the North American crustaceans (I'm biased, I admit), but also the most beautiful. When cooked, Dungies, as they are affectionately known, are readily identified by their brilliant sunset-orange shells. But a live Dungeness crab is dressed in a rainbow of color: it's carapace (the upper shell) a dusky violet; the legs streaked with orange; the claws look to be fashioned of ivory, the "shoulders" tinted deep magenta, and the "armpits," if you can call them that, are as blue as the sea.

Dungeness crab live in the chilly waters of the Pacific Ocean, from as far south as Santa Barbara north to Alaska, but the heart of their range is northern Washington. Which makes the Port Angeles seaside the most obvious place to host the annual Dungeness Crab and Seafood Festival.

◇◇◇◇◇◇◇◇◇◇◇◇◇◇◇◇◇

Port Angeles's inaugural festival was held in 2001, and it was established, like all food festivals, to celebrate local flavors and to raise awareness of (and money for) the community. You'll find the typical festival stuff at this annual event, such as local music, craft stands, food vendors, informational booths, demonstrations, and a large tent filled with picnic tables for hundreds of strangers to gather and greet one another, make small talk, and eat communally. One notable distinction is revealed in the festival's tagline, and it is seen on every sign and read on every flyer by festival goers, revealing the larger movement that's afoot: Celebrating Olympic Coast Cuisine.

Neil Conklin, who owns Bella Italia restaurant in downtown Port Angeles, was an early champion of crafting and defining a distinctive cuisine for the region, similar to the cuisine of the larger Pacific Northwest, but one that focuses on flavors from the sea; the Salish Sea, to be specific. Neil was featured in that article I mentioned in the prologue, the one in which Hsiao-Ching Chou wistfully yearned for satellites of American cuisine. Chou asked Conklin how he defines Olympic cuisine. "It starts with the community crab feed," he answered. Which is what the Dungeness Crab Festival was in those early years. As Conklin expanded his definition of Olympic cuisine, it sounded awfully like the larger PNW region's food. But in time, the festival has grown. And with it, Olympic Coast cuisine has been clarified as something more distinct.

One of the best things about Port Angeles's annual food festival is the opportunity for local chefs and food purveyors to come together and meet famous colleagues from around the region or further afield. Graham Kerr, the *Galloping Gourmet*, was a fixture at the festival for many years. Other prominent chefs from the greater region are booked each year. It provides opportunity for the local chefs, farmers, fishermen, and distrib-

The festival site in downtown Port Angeles, with the majestic Olympic mountains looking on.

utors to speak with these visiting chefs with established celebrity and to learn from one another, furthering their goal of creating a satellite cuisine (to use Chou's words) that is distinct from that of the larger Pacific Northwest.

When I attended the fourteenth annual Dungeness Crab and Seafood Festival, the distinction of Olympic Coast cuisine was already apparent. There were locally grown vegetables and herbs and artisan cheeses from boutique dairies, along with craft beer and what not. But the foundation of every meal was the unique bounty of mollusks and crustaceans and fish caught right off the shores of the Dungeness Valley. And the cornerstone of this burgeoning cuisine is the reason this California epicure was in town.

HOW TO COOK A CRAB

I was curious how folks up here on the Olympic Peninsula prepare their Dungeness crab: Boiled or steamed? Whole or cluster?

Quinton Chastain checks the temperature of a simmering pot of Dungeness crabs.

(The latter refers to breaking down and cleaning the crab, leaving the legs and the rib meat intact.) I quickly discovered there wasn't consensus. Many pointed to the tradition of boiling them live and whole. But in the words of one festival-goer, "Tradition is quaint, but it ain't always right."

I approached a young, bearded, barrel-bodied man standing over a steaming cauldron. He had a thermometer in one hand and a pitchfork in the other. "Two more minutes," I heard him yell to his crew. Quinton Chastain has been involved with the Dungeness Crab Festival since its inception. For the past three years, he's held the title of crab derby coordinator—the overseer of a crab fishing contest in which patrons try to catch specially tagged Dungies to win prizes. (They can then have their prized catch cleaned, cooked, and wrapped for a modest one-dollar donation.) But today, Chastain is manning the crab pots. With heaping mounds of flailing crustaceans behind him and hungry festival-goers in front, Chastain was very busy.

Nevertheless, Chastain was gracious and found time to share his thoughts on the proper manner of cooking crab in the PNW. At the festival, he was boiling whole crab in salted water—pretty standard, I thought. So, I asked for a bit more detail, hoping to learn if there was anything particular about the water. "How much salt do you add? Do you use any other seasonings?" That's when Quinton proudly boasted of the true Pacific Northwest tradition of cooking Dungeness crab.

"The rule of thumb is, add enough salt until it tastes like the sea," he said. "But that's pointless when the sea is right outside your front door." Indeed, why fill a pot with treated (and possibly chlorinated and fluoridated) tap water and then dump in a bunch of iodized salt? All self-respecting crabbers and cooks up here on the peninsula cook their crabs in the very same harbor, strait, or bay water from which the crabs were caught. There's no need for Old Bay or any other ancillary seasoning. Any nuance in flavor one might taste between a crab pulled from the Strait of Juan de Fuca and one caught off the Pacific Coast or in Puget Sound could be attributed to the unique flavors of those distinct waters. Some are saltier than others, or have more aquatic life, or different populations of sea plants. The difference in the final cooked crab would likely be small, but I found the imagery provocative, nonetheless.

"But I prefer not to use water at all," Quinton admitted, which caught me by surprise. Instead, he uses beer. "Any particular kind?" I asked. He immediately answered Olympia, which at one time was the local brew. (It's now brewed in Southern California, and is no longer made with artesian water). "But any light, American-style lager will do," he said. Whenever Chastain and his girlfriend crave crab, he'll run down to the local brewery and pick up a couple growlers, enough to boil two crabs with a couple of pints leftover to wash them down.

When I thought about boiling beer, I envisioned an expanding, bubbling brew overflowing the stock pot, creating quite a mess. I asked Quinton about this, and he shared yet another tip. He never brings his water (or beer) to a rolling boil. Even at the festival, Chastain brings the seawater to 165°F and then simmers the crabs until an internal temperature of 145°F is reached. If cooking one crab, that might take as little as five minutes, Chastain said. For the festival, he cooks forty at a time, which could take as long as half an hour.

Quinton had to return to his duties; it was time to check the temperature of another batch of crabs. He checks one crab, then another, and then a third. Done. He grabs his pitchfork and shovels the now radiant orange crabs into large blue bins, telling volunteers to cover them immediately with ice to halt the cooking. When cool enough to handle, another crew of volunteers begin the messy task of cracking and cleaning the Dungies. Piles of freshly cleaned clusters were then rushed to the central tent where the hungry revelers awaited.

Quinton shows off a batch of seawater-simmered Dungeness crabs.

As I stood in line for my meal, I heard some of the locals proclaim their preference for steamed Dungeness crab, not boiled (or even simmered). And many others said they crack and clean their crabs before cooking. But at the festival's crab feed, you get crabs cooked Quinton's way. And I couldn't find any reason to complain.

HOW TO EAT A CRAB

I sat down at a table under the tent with my festival dinner: Chastain's seawater-simmered crab cluster, an ear of sweet corn, drawn butter, and a cup of rich, silky crab bisque. Now something to drink. Wine or beer up here? I chatted with a couple of seniors who were sitting with me and they immediately said wine; chardonnay to be specific. The young hipster across from me disagreed. "What? No, no, no," he chimed in. "Wine is for Californians. On the Olympic Peninsula, we drink beer." He had a point. When I looked around the festival, I spotted far more beer drinkers (and coffee drinkers) than wine drinkers. But that didn't deter the senior couple, who admitted they were from Victoria and took the ferry across the strait for the festival. "Well, we're not from California, but in Canada, we know a thing or two about Dungeness crab also, and let me tell you, wine is what you should drink." The young man shook his head and smiled in mock disgust. It was friendly, good-natured ribbing by representatives of two different generations from two different countries. Moments like these remind me why I love food festivals so much.

I then asked my neighbors which part of the crab was better: the claws, legs, or rib meat? No strong opinions here, except for my own. I think of Dungeness crab meat akin to chicken. The rib meat is like the chicken breast of the crab; the whitest and lightest meat, but also the blandest. The legs, however, are a bit firmer, chewier, with more assertive flavor. This meat is darker (again, think chicken) because they begin to take on some of that red-orange color of the exoskeleton after it's been cooked. But the claw meat is far and away the best. This is where you find the firmest meat, with the sweetest flavor and darkest color. Sometimes, the claw is almost completely dyed burnt orange, the pigments of the shell staining the white meat. Breaking the claw and then teasing out the meat takes determination, though. (Which is why I think many favor the rib meat, as there is little work required to access that part of the crab.) But the sweet reward hidden in those claws is well worth the effort.

My meal was hearty and tasty, if a bit pedestrian. While drawn butter is a staple condiment with Dungeness crab, I find it a bit too sweet, so I forewent that. Besides, I buttered my sweet corn, and that was sufficient to add a layer of sweet fat to my crab cluster. I'll choose a crisp chardonnay (that's the California in me) over a buttery one for the same reason. It's easy to

My dinner at the fourteenth annual Dungeness Crab and Seafood Festival.

overwhelm the delicate crab flavor with the accompaniments; the dish can get too buttery and sweet. Here, less is more.

The best part of any food festival, though, is visiting the many vendors and discovering the creative dishes local eateries concoct with the featured ingredient. At Sergio's Hacienda, you can choose between Dungeness crab enchiladas or Dungeness crab and baby shrimp ceviche served in a hot tostada. The Cedars at Dungeness serves up Canadian greasy spoon fare, like their Dungeness crab poutine. (If you haven't had it, poutine originated in Quebec and is traditionally a plate of French fries and cheese curds topped with gravy. Here, fresh, steamed Dungeness crab is added under the gravy.) The town's stalwart eatery—the Port Angeles Crab House—serves up perfect Northwest comfort food in the form of Dungeness crab mac 'n' cheese. Crab cakes are the obvious specialty at the Dungeness Crab Cake Co., while Friends of the Fields served up a lip-smacking Dungeness crab quiche that enticed me to return for seconds. (I discovered Dungeness crab and eggs to be an utterly sublime flavor pairing.)

But my blue ribbon for both crab flavor and creativity would go to Blondie's Plate, an eatery in neighboring Sequim which specializes in tapas-style portions. Their Dungie shooters—a one-ounce "shot" of steamed crab with a choice of seasonings—showcased the versatility of Dungeness crab in ways that surprised me and even some of the most seasoned chefs at the festival. Kim McDougal, Blondie's Plate's proprietor, set out three variations for us to try: Bloody Mary and celery, finger lime caviar and cilantro, and ginger-wasabi aioli with pickled cucumbers. All were fabulous, but my personal favorite was the finger lime and cilantro. I always think of citrus with fish, except with Dungeness crab, for some reason. But that bracing acidity of the Australian lime was the perfect foil to the crab's sweet meat, and both were highlighted by the fresh, green brightness of cilantro. Years later, I still think about that bite of food. It is easily the most exciting Dungeness crab preparation I've ever tasted.

HOW TO KILL A CRAB

The pleasures of eating Dungeness crab are obvious to the seafood lover, and I find cooking it enjoyable, even meditative at times. But any gastronome who truly prizes flavor and freshness will, sooner rather than later, come face-to-face with this creature they are about to eat. Nothing ruins a meal quicker than to talk in detail about how the succulent, sweet fish we are about to taste was slaughtered and gutted. But the more I speak with the fishermen, fishmongers, and chefs who also prize flavor and freshness, the more I realize one of the most important steps in the preparation of Dungeness crab is how and when the creature is killed. Not just out of concern for the discriminating diner, but out of respect for the animal as well.

The most common method of killing a live crab is dropping it into a pot of boiling, salted water. This is how it's done at the Dungeness Crab Festival, and justifiably so. When hordes of hungry patrons clamor for fresh Dungeness crab, efficiency becomes necessity. Thousands of pounds of crab are consumed during that weekend, and Chastain has little choice but to dump the crustaceans into simmering cauldrons by the shovelfuls. Though this is the traditional manner of killing and cooking Dungeness crab, some argue it doesn't yield the best flavor.

Dungeness crabmeat is delicate—sweet, light, clean, but consequently, easily masked. Cooking live crabs whole means the gills, viscera, and excreta are cooked along with the white meat. The internal organs and intestinal waste have more intense flavor (which is prized by a few seafood gourmands), and that flavor is leached into the water and then infused into the white meat. It's not that boiling live crabs whole isn't a delicious way to prepare them; it is. But it's impossible to highlight pure crabmeat flavor in a dish if it is boiled along with the guts and poop.

Boiling crabs alive may also be excruciatingly painful. We cooks and diners like to believe as soon as the crustaceans hit that 212°F water, they instantly die. Except that most cooks in the know, like Chastain, don't bring their water to rolling boil, but a burbling simmer. Dungeness crabs can survive through a wide temperature continuum, from very frigid waters to those that are quite warm. At 165°F, the water is obviously well beyond the creature's physiology to survive, but there is some time lapse before the nervous system goes into full arrest. I have spoken with chefs who say a live crab will squirm violently for a few seconds when they are dropped into the hot water. And crabs will sometimes self-amputate their legs and claws in a drastic attempt to flee the pain. At the very least, the crab's muscles tense tightly when it is dropped into the boiling water, and many chefs believe this yields tougher meat.

Another popular method of killing a crab, especially among fishermen, is half-backing. The technique ensures a quick death and carries the bonus of cleaving the crab in half and separating the viscera from the rib meat in one fluid motion. However, the kill is violent and certainly not for the squeamish.

Half-backing (some also call it live-backing) begins by grabbing a Dungeness crab by its legs, so it won't pinch you. The right hand grabs the five right legs and the left hand the left legs. Rap the crab's face sharply against the edge of a rock, dock, gunwale (the top edge of a boat hull), or a kitchen counter. The carapace will fly off the back of the crab, along with some viscera. With the crab still held firmly, snap the breastplate in half, then shake each hand sharply downward. The remaining viscera and gills will fly from the rib meat. The complete technique takes three seconds for the experienced, and the result is a perfectly cleaned and cleaved Dungeness crab. The downside (aside from the violence) is the mess.

As I said, this is a favorite of fishermen, who can catch dozens of crabs in their traps on every outing. Selling crabs to markets that only want the legs means these crustaceans need to be killed and cleaned expeditiously. Half-backing is often done on the boat or at the dock, where the guts can be flung back into the water, providing food for the rest of the marine environment while minimizing cleanup. The carcass halves can then be quickly swished through the seawater, flushing the last bits of viscera still clinging to the meat.

Some chefs prefer to use a knife or cleaver to kill Dungeness crabs. A live crab is placed onto the chopping block, and a blade is driven right between its eyes and through its carapace. This technique is cleaner than half-backing and delivers a quick death, but only if you're confident and accurate.

For the timid home cook who doesn't have much experience handling or killing food of any sort, one of the easiest methods of crab slaughter is also the cleanest and most humane. But it requires a lesson in crab anatomy.

The Dungeness crab's nervous system is relatively simple. While they don't have a brain the way we think of one, they have a nerve center; two of them, actually. One is near the mouth and the other is in the abdomen, right under an abdominal flap called the "apron." Piercing both nerve centers with a chef's knife, quickly and decisively, has been deemed the least painful for the crab, by both The Humane Society and the Royal Society for the Prevention of Cruelty to Animals. But first, the animal should be sedated.

When Dungeness crabs are exposed to very cold temperatures for prolonged periods of time, they enter a state of torpor; they are alive, but numb and insensible. They are also immobile, which alleviates anxiety we might have about handling a live crab with ten legs and two very strong claws. So, the first step in humanely killing a crab is to place it in your freezer.

Depending on the vigor of your particular crab, one hour in the freezer should be sufficient to render the crab unconscious. To confirm, look at its eyes or tap its mouth. If no movement can be discerned, your crab is in a state of deep sleep. Flip it onto its back, and look for the apron on the abdomen; a flap in the under shell shaped like an obelisk or phallus. (At least, this is the apron's shape for males, which for reasons of conservation, is the only gender of Dungie allowed to be harvested.) Lift the tip of the apron, and look for a tiny hole or slit in the soft belly tissue. This is the gateway to the hind nerve center. Take your chef's knife, place the tip into that diminutive opening, and drive it home. Quickly remove the knife, and look for a small depression under the crab's mouth. Under that depression is the front nerve center. Again, place the tip of the knife into the depression, and stab through. With both nerve centers pierced, the crab has been killed with minimal suffering, and is now ready to be cleaned, steamed, and enjoyed.

CLAMS, CRABS, AND THE BIRDS

One morning in the summer of 1961, hundreds of crazed birds attacked the seaside town of Capitola, California. The birds cried like babies as they dove into street lamps, crashed through glass windows, and attacked people on the ground. Most of the birds were sooty shearwaters, a normally non-aggressive species that feeds on small fish and comes ashore only to breed. This incident fascinated Alfred Hitchcock, who frequently vacationed in nearby Santa Cruz. He included newspaper clippings about the Capitola attack in his studio proposal for THE BIRDS, which appeared in cinemas two years later. The agent responsible for the attack is now widely thought to have been domoic acid.

I found this interesting factoid as I was combing the website of Washington's Department of Fish and Wildlife, looking for answers to a puzzling event that shut down Dungeness crab fisheries up and down the West Coast in 2015. If you're a resident of Northern California, Oregon, or Washington, you know how important Dungies are to the economy and cuisine of your state. They are a seasonal delicacy that many of us on the West Coast look forward to as fall sets in and the holiday season approaches. A favorite Thanksgiving-time meal in the Bay Area is steamed Dungeness crab—preferably purchased at San Francisco's Fisherman's Wharf—served with drawn butter, sourdough bread fermented with the native yeasts, and a crisp Napa or Sonoma chardonnay; simple but soulful, and distinctly San Franciscan.

But Bay Area traditionalists had to tweak their recipe in 2015. We could still buy Dungeness crab at Fisherman's Wharf, but these crustaceans weren't caught just outside the Golden Gate, as we've come to expect. Nor were they Californian, or even Oregonian Dungies. At every fishmonger, grocery store, and seafood restaurant throughout California and Oregon, the story was the same: the Dungeness crab was imported from . . . *Washington*?

I was crushed. Just earlier that year I attended the Port Angeles Dungeness Crab Festival and spent three days eating every Dungie dish food vendors dreamed. I returned to California with newfound zeal for Dungeness crab, but I'd had my fill of the Washington variety. The crab season was about to start in California, and I couldn't wait to taste our local Dungies, eager to compare their flavor and firmness with those in the PNW. But that year, foodies out west were given a tough-love lesson on harmful algal blooms, shellfish toxicity, and something called domoic acid.

Domoic acid is a neurotoxin produced by certain marine algae when environmental conditions are ripe for these harmful algal blooms. Bivalves, such as oysters, mussels, and clams, help filter the sea as they consume phytoplankton, trapping contaminants and toxins, if they are present, in their flesh. Some toxins, like domoic acid, don't appear to have any ill effects on these mollusks. Nor does it seem to harm fish or crustaceans—like Dungeness crabs—who eat the bivalves. For mammals and birds, however, ingesting fish and shellfish with large concentrations of domoic acid can be fatal.

Even in lower doses, domoic acid can wreak havoc on the brain and nervous system. Humans get dizzy and confused, and we lose our short-term memory; sea lions and seals go into fits and spasms; and ordinarily quiet, docile sea birds shriek and fly into street lamps, crash through windows, and dive-bomb humans. Scarier still, there is no antidote to domoic acid. Wholesale avoidance of affected seafood is the only safeguard to marine and public health.

But why were Washington Dungies safe to eat? What is different about that ecosystem that prevents domoic acid production? I asked Don Velasquez and Don Rothaus, two biologists at Washington's Department of Fish and Wildlife, for some insight. "To clarify," Velasquez said, "Dungeness crab caught off Washington's western shore also tested positive for domoic acid. The Washington crab you saw in the grocery store likely came from Puget Sound, the San Juan archipelago, or off the coast of Port Angeles and Dungeness, in the Strait of Juan de Fuca."

Velasquez and Rothaus then explained marine trophic levels to me—the food chain starting with phytoplankton, those first level organisms that consume sunlight, followed by zooplankton that consume phytoplankton, bivalves that consume phytoplankton and zooplankton, crabs that consume bivalves, birds and mammals that consume crabs, and so on. Razor clams—another mollusk native to the Pacific Northwest, like geoduck, only smaller—thrives along Washington's Pacific coast. These clams, like all bivalves, are known to marine biologists as first level accumulators. As I mentioned, bivalves filter enormous quantities of seawater as they consume phytoplankton (like algae), and in so doing, accumulate in their flesh any toxins that might be present. Any organism that feeds on these first level accumulators, such as crabs, would absorb and accumulate those toxins as well. The primary food source for Washington's Pacific coast Dungies are razor clams. If domoic acid isn't present in razor clams, then obviously it won't be detected in Dungeness crab. But that was not the case in 2015. That year, commercial and recreational razor clamming were shut down because high concentrations of domoic acid were detected in the mollusk. Which led to the shuttering of the Dungeness crab season as well.

But razor clams are scarce in the Strait of Juan de Fuca and Puget Sound. These mollusks need high-energy shorelines with turbid water, like that of the pounding Pacific surf. The strait waters and the Sound are calmer, creating a different ecosystem. The Dungies living in these waters thus eat different first level accumulators. And they don't feast predominantly on one species of bivalve, Rothaus noted, but all sorts of mollusks, and barnacles and other small crustaceans, too. They will even scavenge dead fish. And because recreational fishing is so popular in the Sound and along the more protected areas in the strait, Dungeness crab in those waters consume an assortment of fish bait.

Diet aside, the core reason Dungies from Washington's more inland, protected waters were safe to eat in 2015 was because the Strait of Juan de Fuca, Puget Sound, and the San Juan archipelago are "immune to domoic acid events," according to Velasquez, because "the algal community is so different." Variables like water temperature, freshwater concentration, and the presence of ferrous metals have a profound effect on domoic acid production. The exact conditions that spawned the harmful algal blooms up and down the West Coast in 2015 have never been present in the straits and Puget Sound.

In 2016, elevated levels of domoic acid were again detected in Dungeness crab along the Northern California coast, and the crabbing season was delayed. For the Bay Area, it meant another Thanksgiving without local Dungies. As I write this mid-autumn of 2017, biologists have found yet again elevated levels of domoic acid in Dungeness crab caught off California's North Coast. It's too early to say whether these elevated levels will hamper the Northern California Dungie season for the third straight year or if domoic acid will affect the Oregon and Washington coast fisheries. Nevertheless, the bigger issue is the neurotoxin is occurring with alarming regularity. Some point to climate change as the culprit. Whatever the reason, what used to be an aberration in the ecosystem along the West Coast is looking like a perennial concern.

If that proves to be the case, at least I know a special locale where I can get one of my favorite holiday foods. Until biology proves otherwise, eating Dungeness crab from the waters off Port Angeles and Dungeness—from the very locale where these crustaceans were named—should calm a nervous mind and sate a rumbling stomach hungry for this crustacean's light, succulent, delicately sweet meat.

DUNGENESS CRAB RECIPES

The Dungeness Crab Festival in Port Angeles offers the seafood lover a delectable variety of Dungie and fish dishes under one roof (or in this case, a tent). The standard is boiled crab, which is tasty on its own. Other familiar preparations included a silky Dungeness crab bisque and an absolute gobble-worthy crab quiche. There were also a few distinctive concoctions, some culturally inspired, that paired crab with foreign ingredients I never would have thought to use.

I've included a trio of recipes for what I consider the standout dishes of the fourteenth annual Crab Fest. One of those recipes, the quiche, taught me Dungeness crab and eggs can be an exquisite pairing. When I returned home from the festival, I went to work perfecting my omelet and then folding in fresh herbs and barely warm, fresh Dungeness claw meat. To this day, I don't think I've had a more sublime breakfast.

DUNGENESS CRAB BISQUE

(Makes 8 servings)

Recipe courtesy of Toga Hertzog, Toga's Soup House

Toga Hertzog is another fine PNW chef who firmly believes in killing Dungeness crab right before cooking and then separating the meat and viscera. When I asked him for his recipe for the rich, silken bisque he prepares at the festival, he first detailed the importance of killing and prepping the crab before even thinking of starting the soup stock. "It's not like I find pleasure in killing live animals," Hertzog said. "I just believe certain food like seafood tastes best when fresh, and nothing gets fresher than killing a crab right before you cook it."

What makes Toga's recipe stand out, however, is his use of the entire animal. It's a delicious way to pay homage to a creature we are about to eat, while demonstrating the unique flavor inherent in every part of the crab's anatomy—the carapace, viscera, and claws. Cooking crab this way adds deep and layered flavor to an otherwise straightforward soup.

The quantities of ingredients Hertzog needs to feed the thousands of festival goers is dizzying. (He said he uses about two-and-a-half tons of Dungeness crab, and makes about 130 gallons of soup!) I've done my best to reduce his festival recipe to something more manageable for a typical household, but please, adjust the seasonings and quantities to suit your taste.

INGREDIENTS

Crab Stock

(Note: you will have stock left over)

8 cups water
4 tablespoons sea salt
2 tablespoons granulated white sugar
1 live Dungeness crab

Bisque

3 cups crab stock (you will only use a portion of the stock)
1 cup half-and-half
2 cups 40% heavy whipping cream
1 cup 2% milk
1 6-ounce can tomato paste
½ tablespoon granulated sugar
¾ teaspoon paprika powder
1 tablespoon onion powder
1 tablespoon garlic powder
1 tablespoon garlic, minced
⅓ cup dry sherry
⅓ cup cornstarch
¼ cup fresh chives, parsley, tarragon, or chervil, minced

PREPARATION

Crab Stock

Begin by killing the crab, preferably employing the "chef's knife to the nervous system" method (see "How to Kill a Crab" on page 107). Remove the carapace then break the crab in half with your hands and shake the two halves downward into a large bowl. The viscera will fall away from the rib meat and into the bowl. Next, scoop out the gills and remaining innards, placing all of this into the bowl as well. Rinse off the remaining bits from the crab meat, and set aside. (Hertzog says the rule of thumb is to remove everything that isn't pure white; the white stuff is the crab meat.)

Fill a stock pot with the water, salt, and sugar and bring to a boil. Drop in the cleaned crab and cook for 10 minutes. Meanwhile, prepare an ice bath in another large bowl. Remove the crab halves from the stock pot and immediately plunge into the ice bath to halt the cooking. Allow the crab to cool for 15 minutes, then remove.

Place the carapace, gills, and viscera into the same stock pot the crab was just cooked in and boil for a minimum of 15 minutes, or until the desired color, flavor, and quantity of stock is achieved. (Reducing the stock yields a deeper color and more concentrated crab flavor.) Strain through a chinois to ensure all shell fragments are removed from the stock.

Bisque

Grab a large sauce pan (a 4-quart is sufficient) and whisk 2 cups of the crab stock with the half-and-half, whipping cream, milk, tomato paste, sugar, paprika, onion powder, garlic powder, and minced garlic. Heat gently over low heat until just boiling. Now whisk in the sherry and cornstarch to thicken.

Taste the bisque and add more stock if desired. Add a bit more cornstarch, too, if needed. The bisque should coat a wooden spoon and run off in a silky texture. While the soup is heating, crack the crab legs and claws and remove the meat. Mix the leg meat with the rib meat and add to the warm bisque.

Ladle the bisque into warm soup bowls, sprinkle the surface with fresh herbs, and serve with a light lager or a crisp chardonnay.

DUNGENESS CRAB QUICHE

(Makes 8 servings)

This incredibly yummy quiche comes courtesy of Michael Wall, the founder of Raindrop Desserts, a gourmet dessert bakery in Port Angeles. Wall bakes these pies for the festival on-site and sells them at the Friends of the Field booth, an organization that supports local farmers. When I had seen how long the line was at the booth, I figured Wall was cooking up something special. And my intuition was spot on.

What I noticed immediately was the focused flavor of the disparate ingredients. The quiche was eggy and cheesy, as good quiche is, yet the crab flavor still came through with tantalizing clarity. I'm not generally a fan of potatoes with fish or eggs or pastry of any sort; but in Wall's recipe, they complement the crab and crust and quiche filling amazingly well.

Of all the food vendors I had visited and dishes sampled that weekend, Wall's was the only one I came back to for seconds.

Recipe courtesy of Michael Wall, Raindrop Desserts

INGREDIENTS

1 9-inch pie shell (See page 78)

½ cup peeled Yukon gold or yellow potato, ¼- to ½-inch dice (avoid Russets, as they get too soft and mushy after even a quick parboil)

½ cup yellow onion, chopped

1½ teaspoons avocado, grapeseed, canola, or other neutral flavored oil

4 large eggs

1½ cups half-and-half

½ ounce crab base

Salt and pepper, if necessary

6 ounces Dungeness crab meat

6 ounces parmesan cheese, grated

Italian seasoning

PREPARATION

Start with your favorite pie crust. It's probably Grandma's, but maybe you prefer Mom's, Betty Crocker's, or even Trader Joe's.

For me, I use Kate McDermott's recipe, since she is the master of pie in the Pacific Northwest. The same dough she uses for her scrumptious Geoduck Deep-Dish Pie (see page 76) is perfect for this Dungie quiche. Par bake the pie crust according to the recipe (or package instructions), then let cool.

Begin preparing the quiche filling by parboiling the peeled and diced potatoes. You don't want them too soft—just until al dente, or still firm—because they will cook a bit more while the quiche bakes. Sweat the onions in oil over medium-low heat until soft. Remove the onions and potatoes from the stove when done and allow to cool.

Next, whisk the eggs, half-and-half, and crab base in a medium bowl, making sure that the crab base is fully dissolved. Taste before adding any additional salt or pepper, as soup bases can be on the salty side.

In a large bowl, toss together the potato, onion, crab meat, and parmesan and pour into the pie shell. Ladle the liquid ingredients over, being careful not to overfill. (Depending on the actual dimensions of your 9-inch pie-shell, you may have some liquid left over).

Sprinkle the top with Italian seasoning and bake at 350°F until the quiche is set, about 50 minutes (or until a knife inserted into the center of the quiche comes out clean). Let the quiche cool for a few minutes, then slice into 8 pieces and serve.

DUNGENESS CRAB SHOOTERS

(Makes 20 shooters)

Recipe courtesy of Chef Carlos H. Osorio Jr., Blondie's Plate

One booth caught my attention not for the crab but for the produce. Kim McDougal, the owner of Blondie's Plate, was talking excitedly to a visitor about finger limes. Finger limes excite me, too. This citrus caviar, as Kim described it, is a delight to feel on the tongue, with the gentlest of bites bursting the tiny pearls and flooding the mouth with bracing acidity. McDougal then touted how wonderful this native Australian fruit paired with the local Dungeness crab. It was then I noticed dozens of 1-ounce plastic cups filled with a single bite of shredded crab topped with an amazing variety of produce and condiments.

McDougal wasn't showcasing the pure flavor of Dungeness crab, but rather its incredible versatility. Finger lime, ginger-wasabi aioli, and pickled cucumbers and carrots were just a few fun ingredients that I never thought would complement Dungeness crab, yet they did so fabulously. The Blondie's booth was easily the most exciting for me, because Kim and her chef Carlos taught me new flavor tips.

INGREDIENTS

2 pounds Dungeness crab meat, cooked and finger shredded

Bloody Mary and Celery

1 celery stalk with leaves
1 cup tomato juice
1 tablespoon lemon juice
1 tablespoon lime juice
1 teaspoon prepared horseradish
1 teaspoon Worcestershire sauce
1 teaspoon garlic, minced
Tabasco, to taste
1 teaspoon salt
Pinch freshly ground pepper
Giardiniera brine, to taste

Pickled Cucumber and Carrot with Ginger-Wasabi Aioli

1 small cucumber, skin-on, seeds removed, brunoise cut
1 carrot, brunoise cut
2 cups rice wine vinegar
1 egg
1⅓ cups neutral flavored oil, like canola, grapeseed, or avocado
1 tablespoon Dijon mustard
1⅓ teaspoons pickled ginger juice
2 teaspoons pickled ginger
Wasabi powder, to taste

Finger Lime with Citronette and Cilantro

⅔ cup lemon juice
1 cup olive oil
1½ tablespoons honey
1½ tablespoons white vinegar
2 teaspoons dry tarragon
1 teaspoon salt

1 teaspoon freshly ground
 black pepper
6 finger limes, sliced in half on
 a bias
2 sprigs fresh cilantro

PREPARATION

Place 1½ to 2 ounces of crab meat in a shot glass, or any small vessel you want to serve the bite from. Top each portion with one of the following condiments. (You will have leftover toppings.)

Bloody Mary and Celery

Remove the celery leaves and chiffonade. Mince the celery stalk and set aside.

Whisk the remainder of the ingredients together—this will be the Bloody Mary mix. Pour just one-half ounce of mix into each shot glass, and reserve the rest for a real Bloody Mary. Top each shooter with a bit of the celery stalk and leaves.

Pickled Cucumber and Carrot with Ginger-Wasabi Aioli

Place equal parts of the finely diced cucumber and carrot in a bowl. Mix well and cover with rice wine vinegar. Allow the veggies to pickle for at least 24 hours.

In a food processor, puree the egg and Dijon mustard for 1 minute. Slowly drizzle in the oil with the processor running. As the mixture starts to thicken and resemble mayonnaise, slowly incorporate the pickled ginger juice and the pickled ginger. (If the mixture seems too thick, you can adjust with warm water and/or pickled ginger juice, depending on your taste.) At this time, slowly incorporate the wasabi powder to your personal taste.

Spoon one-half teaspoon of the pickled cucumber and carrot brunoise onto the crab, and top with a dollop of ginger-wasabi aioli.

Finger Lime with Citronette and Cilantro

For the citronette, whisk together the lemon juice, olive oil, honey, vinegar, tarragon, salt, and pepper. Give the crab in each shot glass a squirt of the citronette.

Gently squeeze each half of the finger lime until the fruit pearls just begin to ooze out. Top each shooter with one piece of finger lime and a single, freshly picked cilantro leaf.

DUNGENESS CRAB OMELET

(Makes 1 serving)

As I mentioned in the introduction, I first discovered the harmonious flavor of fresh fish and chicken eggs in Seattle near Pike's Place Market, where fresh Chinook salmon and scrambled eggs were staple breakfast fare. Sausage and eggs, bacon and eggs, ham and eggs; these are all fine pairings. But to my palate, pigs and eggs fall flat compared to the melodious union of salmon and eggs, trout and eggs, or—my personal favorite—Dungeness crab and eggs. I thank Pacific Northwesterners for introducing me to their various native fishes and their regional spin on an American breakfast classic.

During the short, gloomy days of winter, when you have the time, try making the Dungeness crab quiche. But when you need a simple and quick breakfast, but one loaded with soul-filling flavor and palate-pleasing texture, this omelet should be your wintertime go-to.

INGREDIENTS

2 claws Dungeness crab, cooked (Any part of the crab will do—legs or rib meat. But the meat from the claws has the best color and flavor.)

1 tablespoon sweet cream butter

3 eggs

1 tablespoon whole milk

Sea salt and pepper to taste

1 tablespoon shallot greens, chives, or green onion, chopped

PREPARATION

Break the crab claws and remove the meat. Dice into bite-sized chunks and set aside.

Melt the butter in a 10-inch nonstick skillet over medium-low heat. Meanwhile, whisk the eggs and milk with a fork; the mixture doesn't have to be silky smooth. Once the butter has melted and starts to brown, pour in the beaten eggs. As the edges begin to set, gently push them to the center with a spatula, allowing the uncooked eggs to spill through and fill the skillet again. Do this a couple of times (the whole process takes about 4 to 5 minutes).

Right before you remove the omelet from the skillet, gently fold in the Dungeness crab meat. Tip the skillet over a plate and let the omelet slide out. Sprinkle with salt and pepper and garnish with the freshly chopped herbs.

5

Portland:

BOUNTY IN THE BRAMBLE

Black huckleberries, harvested at four thousand feet in the Salmon-Huckleberry Wilderness near Mount Hood.

◇◇◇◇◇◇◇◇◇◇◇◇◇◇◇◇◇◇

Not long ago, I had a dish with wild black huckleberries and was transported back in time. They had that deep, luscious blue-black fruit flavor that mysteriously disappeared from West Coast blueberries two decades ago. "What happened to blueberries?" I've thought lately. As a child, I remember them being so flavorful and sweet. Now, every time I buy a plastic clamshell packed with those engorged, sumptuously spherical, dusky blue blueberries and burst a few in my mouth, my palate responds, "Insipid, mealy . . . *meh.*" I can't help but channel the spirit of Clara Peller from those Wendy's commercials back in the 1980s: "Where's the beef? The flavor?" But I found it in those huckleberries, rekindling memories of when blueberries weren't just plump and pretty, but delicious, too.

Before that revelatory day I hadn't given huckleberries any consideration. I thought they were synonymous with blueberries—the same fruit, but with a regional sobriquet, like goober is to peanut (or peanut is to groundnut). I learned later that these two types of berries, though related, are distinct, both in flavor and origin. Blueberries, at least the kind we typically eat, hail from New England. Huckleberries are indigenous to the Pacific Northwest.

I was planning a summer trip up through Oregon and over to the coast when I came across an announcement for a berry festival in Portland. This festival was largely a celebration of the familiar commercial berries—strawberries, blueberries, raspberries, blackberries—but I thought, why not plan my trip around that event? Maybe I'll learn something about Oregon's berry industry. Better yet, maybe I'll get another taste of wild huckleberries.

The one-day festival was quite modest in size. I parked my car in a public garage and walked through the Pearl District to a parking lot kitty-corner to Jamison Square, the spot of the annual Oregon Berry Festival. I entered the festival at Tenth and Irving and immediately sought shade. Portland can be quite pleasant in the summer—a welcome respite from the drear and rain that pervades the city the rest of the year. But today the city was sizzling, with temperatures approaching 100°F.

I walked quickly through the parking lot, noting the different berry booths and fresh produce, food and beverage samples, the pamphlets and flyers touting the nutritional benefits of berries, and almost knocked over the person trying hard to look comfortable and cool in that large, overstuffed blueberry costume.

But at the other end of the parking lot, thanks to a few mature street trees, there was shade. Here was the BluesBerry Stage, where music, cooking demonstrations, and lectures would entertain and inform the crowd throughout the day. I sat down to peruse the schedule of events just as Heather Arndt Anderson took the mic.

WHEN LIFE HANDS YOU BERRIES . . .

Arndt Anderson is a culinary historian and author of numerous books, including *Portland: A Food Biography,* and *Berries: A Global History.* Today, she was going to make a huckleberry cake for the crowd. As she mixed the batter, Heather shared a few insights into Oregon's berry history.

She began her history lesson with an important date: 5677 BC (give or take 150 years). That is the year Mount Mazama, a twelve-thousand-foot volcano in the Oregon Cascades, literally blew its top. The volcanic eruption spewed ash and pumice miles into the air, and the prevailing winds spread the tephra far and wide. Mount Mazama imploded, its spout collapsing into the caldera, stunting its elevation by almost a mile. (Today, Mount Mazama is more popularly known by the body of water that collected within the caldera—Crater Lake.)

The volcanic ash blanketed Oregon, Washington, Northern California, Idaho, and western Montana. In time, the ash seeped into the ground, creating a nutrient rich soil with a low pH, the type of soil that supports highly productive forests, like those of the Pacific Northwest. This acidic soil, coupled with the mild winters and cool summers, created the perfect habitat for a host of berries, and dozens of species flourished.

These berries became food staples for the Native Americans in the Pacific Northwest, a source of sustenance and reverence. While corn, beans, and squash were the principal food crops for tribal communities throughout North America, the Three

Sisters of the PNW were salmon, camas root, and huckleberry, according to Arndt Anderson. Months in the Native American calendar were named for the region's most important berries: May after salmonberry, August after salal, September after huckleberry. Then in 1847, a foreigner arrived from the Midwest with some berries of his own.

Henderson Luelling was the Johnny Appleseed of the Pacific Northwest and is considered the father of the Oregon fruit industry. (In Oakland, California, where he is buried, he was given an even loftier title. His tombstone reads: FATHER PACIFIC HORTICULTURE.) He and his wife left their home in Salem, Iowa, and headed for Salem, Oregon, eventually settling just south of Portland. Luelling was a successful nurseryman in Iowa and saw great promise out west. He loaded his wagon with charcoal, manure, soil, and several hundred fruit shrubs and trees: berries, apples, cherries, pears, quince, grapes, plums, and more. He planted his stock in the Willamette Valley, and the fruits thrived. In one account, Luelling tried to teach the Native Americans orcharding techniques and how to use grist mills, but they were not interested in becoming farmers. Conversely, the pioneers flooding into Oregon didn't want to become foragers. As the population of pioneers in Oregon grew, these newcomers, rather than harvesting the fruit intrinsic to the Pacific Northwest, instead chose foreign fruits, more familiar to them. Almost overnight, the bountiful brambles that largely comprise the understory of one of the most productive forests in the Northern Hemisphere were cast aside.

I asked Heather, how did an enterprising horticulturalist like Luelling ignore the fantastic variety of fruits that naturally abounded in the region? Why did the nonnative blueberry become such a huge commercial success in Oregon, while the huckleberry exists as a wild novelty?

"That would have meant reinventing the wheel," she answered. I was confused. The wheel was already here, made strong with spokes of huckleberries, thimbleberries, black raspberries, blackberries, salal, beach strawberries, and salmonberries; a seemingly inexhaustible source of food people here had valued for millennia. Heather clarified:

> True, there was already a culture here of prizing berries. But Luelling had in his possession wagonloads of fruit trees and berry bushes. These plants were the result of the latest in botanical knowledge and technology at the time—hybrids designed to yield many plump, handsome, uniform fruits—even if the flavor was a bit compromised.
>
> By the time hybrid highbush blueberries arrived in western Oregon, it was quick and easy to plant orchards of market-friendly fruit, fruit that could be grown in abundance and shipped all over the continent. The bushes grew upright, so less stooping was required for harvest, and nobody had to hike up the mountains to do so.
>
> Huckleberries would mean starting from scratch.

Arndt Anderson's story of Oregon berries is the story of a great number of original American flavors. During the settling of the United States, newcomers brought the produce with which they were familiar. These foods were cultivated and bred to produce varieties better suited to this foreign landscape. Foods brought from England supplanted those native flavors of New England. And flavors brought from New England supplanted those native flavors of the Pacific Northwest. Regional native flavors that were relished in America for thousands of years were forgotten.

I shared my dismay with Heather, who, as a culinary historian and a fourth-generation Portlander, was sympathetic. I admitted I had hoped to come to the Oregon Berry Festival and discover *true* Oregon berries, those unique to the state. She mentioned one famous Oregonian fruit wildly ballyhooed here at the festival, and pointed to a couple of booths behind me. I thanked her and wandered off, wondering, "What does the former mayor of Washington, DC, have to do with native Oregon fruit?" But silly me, I was confused by a homophone.

THE HONORABLE MARIONBERRY

Oregon is the largest commercial producer of blackberries in the United States, cultivating over fifty varieties for market. Of those dozens of varieties, one blackberry stands out, honored above all its hybridized siblings, parents, and even its own offspring. That berry is the Marion blackberry, commonly marketed as marionberry.

The marionberry hails from Oregon but isn't a native in the sense that it existed in the Oregon wilderness for thousands of years without introduction by humans. Quite the opposite: marionberries are manmade, so to speak, created in 1945 and released to the public in 1956. They are the result of painstaking research and intensive breeding, a collaboration between the USDA's Agricultural and Research Service in Corvallis and Oregon State University. And their lineage is rather fascinating.

In 1881, a California judge and amateur plant breeder named James Logan planted a couple of blackberries in his backyard next to an old raspberry vine. One of the blackberries was an eastern variety, the other a cultivated variety of the native Pacific, or trailing blackberry. The plants crossbred, and one of the seedlings was especially robust. He cultivated that one and named it after himself: loganberry.

Decades later USDA breeder George Waldo crossed the loganberry with a cultivar created in Louisiana by Byrnes Young, the eponymous youngberry. The result of that cross was the olallieberry (*olallie* is the Chinook word for "berry"). Olallieberries never grew well in Oregon, but they thrived in California, so Waldo let it go for a while and focused attention on developing the Chehalem. This blackberry is the result of breeding yet another cultivated variety of the native blackberry (the Santiam) with the Himalaya, a pernicious, thorny weed with incredibly sweet berries, brought into the United States by the famous plant breeder Luther Burbank.

Finally, in 1945, Waldo took his newly created Chehalem, brought back the ollalie, mated the two, and invented the marion. Oregonians immediately fell in love with the berry's generous size, juicy fruit, and sweet, complex flavor. Breeding efforts continue in Oregon, and new blackberry varieties are created, tested, and some eventually brought to market. But marionberries continue to be the most cherished, regarded as Oregon's pinnacle achievement in horticulture. Of the almost fifty million pounds of blackberries produced annually in Oregon, over half is from a single cultivar, the one from Marion County.

◇◇◇◇◇◇◇◇◇◇◇◇◇◇◇◇

One of the most exciting events at the berry festival was a bus trip to Boring. Here we met Julie Schedeen, a farmer who grows an assortment of fruit but specializes in blackberries. Schedeen gave us a tour of her fields, introducing us to all the varieties she and the rest of the Schedeen clan produce. There were boysenberries and loganberries, olallieberries and tayberries; all juicy and lush, but each with a distinctive flavor and color.

Schedeen also grows corn; not for her family or her customers, but for crows. This is a head-scratcher for corn farmers, no doubt. But Schedeen is a berry farmer, and her arch nemesis is the European starling, an invasive habitat wrecker that loves Schedeen's berries. Crows don't ordinarily shoo other birds away, unless they feel their prized cornfield is at risk. By growing a modest amount of corn, the Schedeens (rather, the crows) prevent starlings and other berry-lovin' feathered-frenemies from dining in the berry fields.

We then gathered at the marionberry plot. Schedeen is rightfully proud of all her fruits, but she agrees the marionberry's flavor is hard to beat. She says those in the industry often market these as the "cabernet of blackberries." She invites us to pick a few and taste for ourselves. The fruits are large, slightly conical in shape, longer than they are wide, with a dark, deep purple hue. I pop one in my mouth. The first thing I notice is the flood of juice coating my tongue: easily the juiciest blackberry I've ever tasted.

The berry is sweet, with overtones of typical blackberry tartness. But I also notice how deep the flavor is. I can see why these are favored in pies and muffins and pastries; you want a fruit that maintains clear, assertive flavors after being blended, mixed, and baked. The flavor is also complex, and I immediately understood why it is compared to cabernet sauvignon. I tasted notes of luscious black currant, or crème de cassis, which is an intrinsic essence of the best Bordeaux and California cabernet sauvignon.

Though marionberries are tops in flavor, Schedeen says plant breeders and geneticists still work to create a better blackberry. The one downside of the marionberry is its delicate skin. It lacks the toughness of some its hybridized cousins, meaning the fruits don't transport well. As such, fresh marionberries are somewhat limited to the markets in the Pacific Northwest. She explains, "All breeding efforts strive to create a more marketable blackberry, one that is bigger, juicier, thornless, handsome and uniform in appearance, that ships well with long shelf life. This can be achieved. Then, the breeders try to cap their efforts with the statement, 'With all the flavor of a marionberry.' That's what does them in. No one has succeeded."

THE WILD ONES

After the festival, I thought I'd forage for a few wild berries on my way to the coast. I stopped off at Powell's Books and picked up a couple of field guides. One proved indispensable: *Wild Berries of Washington and Oregon*, coauthored by T. Abe Lloyd. Lloyd is a sixth-generation citizen of the Pacific Northwest and a tireless champion of the region's native foods. He's an ethnobotanist and the founder of Salal, the Cascadian Food Institute, through which he consults with Native American tribal organizations to study and promote indigenous foods. Abe also teaches ethnobotany and leads hands-on foraging courses.

When I returned home and read through my notes on the different berries I found and tasted in Oregon, I discovered some of my flavor impressions were different from the accounts of others. I reached out to Abe, eager to compare his opinions with the notes I had scribbled in my field guides. He graciously responded immediately, and quickly into our conversation I realized I've never spoken with someone more knowledgeable or passionate about berries. Abe was quite the affable geek. We were chatting about some of his favorite berries and he mentioned the nuanced sweetness of the native trailing blackberries. "I'd love to do a phytochemical analysis on those!" he said. Ah yes . . . Abe was a wealth of information, and certainly a joy to speak with.

There are literally dozens of native edible berry species in the PNW, so I asked Lloyd if he could whittle down a core list of his favorites. He didn't hesitate: thimbleberry, Cascade bilberry, and black huckleberry were his top three. Luckily, I was able to find and taste these berries plus a few more during my Oregon trip. For the obvious reason of phenomenal flavor, I found Lloyd's favorites to be mine as well.

When I explained that a few of my flavor impressions were different from those listed in other guides, including his, he explained why that might be. Abe has found when it comes to berries, flavor impressions are skewed because foragers often pluck a fruit that is underripe or overripe. Such are the gastronomic hazards of foraging in the wild. While farmers and chefs may know when, exactly, their produce is at the peak of flavor, most of us would not be able to confidently, consistently pick those fruits that are perfectly ripe.

Adding to the challenge, the evergreen huckleberry, for example, doesn't reach the peak of its deliciousness until after the first frost, and other huckleberries pack more punch at higher elevations. You might find black huckleberries below three thousand feet, but they should really be tasted at higher climbs.

Season and elevation aside, the greatest reason for the different flavor impressions is simply the highly subjective issue of taste. One of the most prevalent wild fruits throughout Oregon is the Oregon grape (*Mahonia aquifolium*). Its blossoms are the state flower of Oregon, and its handsome structure and foliage renders Oregon grape a popular landscaping plant. But most find the fruit of Oregon grape a trailside curiosity. They are very tart, too sharp for most folks' palates, and finish with bitter notes. Unless you are making jam or preserves with copious amounts of sugar—and even then, cutting the sour berries with a sweeter species, like salal (as Lloyd does)—most find the flavor of Oregon grape unpalatable.

But I didn't find Oregon grape any tarter than gooseberries or fresh cranberries. On the contrary, I found their acidity to be cleansing and invigorating, like a tonic, akin to apple cider vinegar. Maybe I got lucky and tasted them at the pinnacle of their ripeness, when there was a greater concentration of sugars. Or maybe I have a predilection for sour grapes. Regardless, palate-puckering cranberries and gooseberries have commercial cachet, as does apple cider vinegar, so I wouldn't pooh-pooh Oregon grape simply because they are sharply acidic.

I do agree that Oregon grape is lower down on the region's list of Most Delicious Berries. This modest list, however, represents the most prized of the native PNW fruits, berries whose sweet and wild flavors are universally adored.

Huckleberries

Huckleberries are the most abundant fruit throughout the PNW, the myriad species adapted to the distinct landscapes of the region. Some species prefer the coast, some the valley, and others the mountains. Some prefer lower elevations, and some higher. Some huckleberries adapted to drier conditions, others boggier. All huckleberries (and their relatives, blueberries and cranberries) belong to the *Vaccinium* genus, and there are thirty-five *Vaccinium* species in North America, fourteen of which are native to the Pacific Northwest. It can be confusing, since common names for these berries sometimes differ by region, but throughout the United States, the *Vacciniums* with dark purple and black fruits are referred to as huckleberries; though if the fruits are blue they are often called blueberries (or bilberries) and if red, they are known colloquially as cranberries. But in the PNW, red, blue, and purple *Vacciniums* are generally known by one moniker: huckleberries.

But the cranberries and blueberries with which Americans are most familiar, the ones we see in supermarkets and farmers markets from California to DC, the Deep South, and even in the Pacific Northwest, are commercial hybrids from distinct species native to the East Coast. The berries highlighted here—four of the best *Vacciniums* one will ever taste—are true PNW natives.

<><><><><><><><><><><><><>

There are many species of huckleberry in and around Portland. The most prevalent, and the one with which most Portlanders are familiar, is red huckleberry (*Vaccinium parvifolium*). I found these in abundance when I was strolling through Hoyt Arboretum. (A must-see attraction, by the way. The views of and from the park are stunning.) Red hucks are shiny and translucent, like red currants, with a sprightly tart flavor akin to cranberries only milder and a touch sweeter. These berries add invigorating acidity and an arresting pop of color to all dishes, from savory appetizers to sweet desserts. (Try pairing red huckleberries with soft, creamy French cow's milk cheeses like camembert and brie.)

Evergreen huckleberries are glossy and very dark purple, bordering on black. Evergreen hucks (*Vaccinium ovatum*—also commonly called California huckleberry) are found in great abundance in the Coast Ranges. These are one of the easiest huckleberries to forage, since they abound in the lowlands, accessible to even the most novice hikers, and are very easy to pick. Large clusters of the glossy berries can be pulled off the vine easily; sometimes shaking a bough over a bucket is the only effort needed.

Evergreen huckleberries are sweet, juicy, and fun to eat because of their snappy texture. Douglas Deur, a professor in the anthropology department at Portland State University and author of *Pacific Northwest Foraging* says evergreen hucks are "juicy on the inside, and very firm on the outside. When bitten, these berries often respond with a satisfying pop." Many insist this berry's best flavor is achieved when it is ripe and touched by a light frost, meaning the upper latitudes will consistently yield the best fruits.

Lloyd's favorite is the Cascade bilberry, also known as Cascade blueberry or blue huckleberry or even blue bilberry. And I can see why. This fruit is the closest in appearance and flavor to a wild Maine blueberry, though he and I argue it's even better. But don't take our word for it. You don't have to speak Latin to understand the reason this berry was given the scientific name *Vaccinium deliciosum*. Cascade bilberries are the sweetest of the PNW berries—*Vacciniums* or otherwise. The flavor is deep and concentrated, and with great balance; like I remember how blueberries used to taste.

A bucket of hucks; black huckleberries on the left, Cascade bilberries on the right. *Courtesy of T. Abe Lloyd*

But most huckleberry fans proclaim the black huckleberry the best, and I count myself in that group. Maybe I rank these fruits higher because Cascade bilberries remind me so much of wild Maine blueberries, whereas black huckleberries (*Vaccinium membranaceum*) seem more exotic simply because their flavor is a bit more distinct. And maybe I consider black hucks superior because I had to work hard for these treats. I got to pluck my first black huckleberries from the bush only after I climbed four-thousand-feet along a narrow trail, then gingerly stepped down a rocky slope to a patch of berries. Or maybe I like black huckleberries best because, as I ate those sweet fruits that tasted like wild blueberries, but with tart notes of raspberry and blackberry, I was deep in the Salmon-Huckleberry Wilderness, ogling a magnificent landscape, staring straight ahead at Mount Hood. Sometimes, the setting is everything.

Black huckleberries currently have the greatest commercial value of the huckleberries, partly because their geographic range is extensive, partly because the plants take over entire hillsides and the fruits are born in great profusion, and largely because of their superb flavor. While they aren't readily found in supermarkets, foragers will often sell truck-beds full of just-picked hucks along the roadsides and at farmers markets throughout the Pacific Northwest.

I consider black huckleberries the perfect introduction to wild foods for those with timorous palates. They look tantalizing, are lusciously sweet, and carry the approval of most everyone who has tasted one. Idahoans love these berries so much, they anointed black huckleberry their state fruit. Indeed, many foragers claim these sumptuous, juicy berries the most delicious, most prized fruit west of the Rockies.

The site of my first black huckleberry forage.

Salal

If there is one fruit that can be the icon of the Pacific temperate rainforest, a fruit that symbolizes not just a landscape but an entire culture, it is salal. Dark purplish-black berries born in bunches on fuzzy, coral pink stems with bright, glossy green leaves makes salal easy to spot among the many understory plants in Oregon's coastal forests. Salal (*Gaultheria shallon*) is the principal fruit along the Pacific Northwest coast and was one of the most important foods for Native Americans in the region. Unlike huckleberry, whose various species can be found throughout the PNW, including Idaho and Montana and even Wyoming, there is but one species of salal and it exists entirely along the coast at low elevations. According to Lloyd, many Coast Salish tribes named the month of August after the ripening of salal berries. But these berries were relished throughout the year; eaten fresh in the summer and then dried and made into cakes for the fall and winter. Salal was also an important trade item, and the foliage was highly useful in fire pit cooking, laid as a protective blanket between the red-hot rocks and whatever root vegetables were going to be roasted. Though salmonberries, thimbleberries, wild strawberries, and trailing blackberries proliferate in the Pacific temperate rainforest, salal was most notable, one of the most useful, and thus, the cornerstone in coastal cuisine long ago.

Salal needs to be perfectly ripe to be enjoyed. If the fruits are a dark and dusky blue with more of an egg shape than a sphere, they are getting close. If the berries are spherical, with glossier, purplish-black skins, and appear to have a starfish deeply embossed on their bottoms, they are getting *really* close to ripe. If the blossom end looks as if the skin of the berry is starting to pull away from the fruit, and you give the berry a tender squeeze with your thumb and forefinger, causing the bottom of the berry to open, unfurling in the shape of a five-petaled flower, *Bingo!* You have a perfectly ripe salal berry.

When salal is ripe, it is juicy and sticky, as a good berry should be. Its flavor is nuanced and complex, tasting akin to a Concord grape, only more floral, with notes of highbush blueberry and black plum. This flavor lingers on the palate, much more so than other berries, and it is this sweet afterglow that I find the most pleasing about this fruit.

My first salal sighting.

Some find the texture a bit pasty or mealy, but Lloyd says that is usually the result of the fruit being slightly overripe. (In defense of salal, I find some varieties of commercial blueberries a bit pasty, as well.) Abe says when they are perfectly ripe, salal is hard to beat for flavor and juiciness, and they can be used in any recipe that otherwise calls for blueberries (or huckleberries).

I will say I found the flavor of salal better the closer I got to the Pacific Ocean. I spoke to Abe about this, and he agreed. Salal needs a maritime influence to develop the best flavor: that dense, wet blanket of fog that keeps the winters mild and the summers cool. It thrives at elevations below one thousand feet, amid the abusive winds howling off the ocean. The best berries are often found within a mile of the breakers.

Salmonberries

I've never been so transfixed by the shimmer and radiance of a berry as I have with salmonberry. It is easily the most captivating of the PNW fruits. Depending on location and season, salmonberries (*Rubus spectabilis*) exhibit a spectacular golden yellow, bright orange, or fiery red sheerness that could easily be mistaken for salmon roe if it weren't sprung from a bramble, hence the name. Others say salmonberries are so named because they ripen at the same time the spring Chinook begin their run in the open sea. Both seem true. Which explains whenever I look at salmonberries, I see more than just food; I see life.

Salmonberry is the first of the PNW berries to ripen once the weather begins to warm, signaling the imminence of summer. Whereas the colors of salmonberries dazzle, their flavor is more muted. These fruits are quite juicy, though some find them a bit watery. But I would describe salmonberry flavor as delicate rather than insipid. The truth is it's hard to pinpoint the flavor of salmonberry, just as it's hard to pinpoint its color. Some salmonberries taste light and bright, borderline citrusy; not unlike their exterior. Other salmonberries have an earthier spice.

I look askance when folks say they don't like salmonberries. The flavor is so variable there is bound to be a berry to suit

Salmonberries, a jubilee of red, orange, and golden yellow.
Courtesy of T. Abe Lloyd

everyone's palate, if they would just taste a few more. But the haters are few. Most find salmonberries pleasant and cleansing, with a juicy freshness evocative of mid-spring.

Salmonberries are quite fragile and always eaten fresh, so you won't find salmonberry muffins or scones. When I was visiting Portland, I sometimes found salmonberries at the bar. These colorful fruits garnished cocktails with a fun pop of color, but their flavor pairs best with neutral spirits, like vodka. But the best salmonberry concoction I've ever had was on a sparsely populated island in the Salish Sea. The berries were served fresh and simply, in a small white porcelain bowl along with beach rose petals and verjus. It was a dish that, in many ways, redefined what "fresh, local ingredients" means to me.

Thimbleberries

As the salmonberry season wanes, thimbleberries arrive in profusion. There is some seasonal overlap, and I found both growing side by side in the Coast Ranges just a half hour west of Portland. Thimbleberries don't possess the glamor of their salmonberry cousin, though they are quite attractive in their own right. What thimbleberries do possess is unrivaled flavor that most argue, including me, is the best of any PNW berry.

Thimbleberry flavor is bracing and shimmery, offering crisp, clean red fruit flavors, balanced by a touch of luscious tropical fruit. Red raspberry is the dominant flavor, but thimbleberries are sweeter, and a touch softer. Raspberries have a certain sharpness that isn't as pronounced in thimbleberries; though, depending on how ripe your thimbleberries are and where you harvest them, you might taste a good dose of acidity. But the thimbleberry's most intriguing flavor is an underlying note of ripe fig. And it is that balanced combination—sweet, luscious fig underlying racy red raspberry flavor—that make thimbleberries the decisive favorite among urban foragers. Marionberries might be the cabernet of blackberries, but thimbleberries are the Champagne of them all.

Another surprising treat are thimbleberry's seeds, something you cannot say about most any other fruit. The seeds are numerous but quite small and brittle, akin to kiwifruit. They disintegrate under the gentlest of bites, and give each berry a delightfully satisfying, toothsome texture—like poppy seeds in a lemon muffin.

When thimbleberries are ripe, they could be mistaken for raspberries at a passing glance, as they exhibit a comparable size and luscious red hue. But your fingers are the best gauge to determine when thimbleberries are ripe. Give a berry a gentle tug; if the cluster pulls off the flower's receptacle easily and cleanly, looking like a tiny red knit beanie, it's time to gorge. But be careful. Thimbleberries are extremely delicate, and need a tender touch when harvesting.

I was discussing thimbleberries with Craig Sailor, a reporter with the *Tacoma News Tribune* and a huge fan of the fruit. Sailor says these berries might be the PNW's greatest wild flavor, at least in the plant kingdom. "But, they are too fragile," he laments. "They have to be eaten direct from the bush and you have to pick them carefully."

That frailty Sailor described is the thimbleberry's Achilles' heel to marketability and thus, popularity. Notable PNW forager Langdon Cook said in his blog, "Thimbles don't have much of a shelf life, like almost zero, usually falling apart in your hand before even hitting your tongue, which is why you never see them for sale. They're a wild treat, meant to be enjoyed in the wild."

When I read Langdon's final pronouncement of the thimbleberry—that it's a wild treat meant to be enjoyed in the wild—I thought, Why? Thimbleberries top Craig Sailor's list of the tastiest fruit in the Pacific Northwest. They top Lloyd's list, and mine, as well. I spoke to many guests at the Oregon Berry Festival and asked them what they considered their favorite wild berry. Anyone who had any experience with wild Oregon berries said the same: nothing beats the flavor and gratifying crunch of a thimble. There is such widespread reverence for this fruit, and consensus of its incredible, unparalleled flavor, that I started to think, Why should this flavor be relegated to the woods? It seems some effort could be made to bring these foods from the wilds to places of domesticity—the supermarket, restaurant, our kitchen pantry—so that Americans can more readily enjoy one of nature's superlative flavors.

The easiest way to bring thimbleberries to a larger audience is through restaurants. Mushrooming, for example, has become lucrative for foragers, while providing chefs with fresh, wild ingredients without any effort from the restaurant staff or its diners. The forager knocking on the back door of the restaurant with a basket of boletes is beyond a quaint figure who might be common in Provence or Tuscany, but a real, widespread practice at the best restaurants up and down the West Coast. I would love to see the same zeal for thimbleberries (and salal,

Thimbleberries, foraged in the Coast Ranges near the Oregon shoreline (and photographed on the hood of my rental car).

and huckleberries, and salmonberries) that PNW chefs have for wild mushrooms.

But there could also be a market beyond white-tablecloth dining. What I learned from the Oregon Berry Festival is that berries are big business, the result of decades of plant breeding and genetic research. Most of this botanical effort is put into creating a more marketable berry—not necessarily one with the best flavor (as it was for the marionberry), but a berry that is more uniform in appearance, sturdier, longer-lived, the characteristics that appeal to supermarkets. I write this today with a recent *New Yorker* article still fresh in my mind. The title of the article is "How Driscoll's Reinvented the Strawberry," with the subtitle "The berry behemoth turned produce into a beauty contest, and won."

We can develop a less fragile thimbleberry, so that it can be enjoyed by millions more Americans. The question that perplexes me is why we are investing so much energy into developing tasteless, dry, mealy strawberries and blueberries (albeit gorgeous ones that last a week or more in our refrigerator), instead of spending some of that energy into bringing such a highly regarded flavor, like thimbleberry, into more homes? After all, this is what led to the breeding of the marionberry.

This sort of discussion and research is exactly what is happening in Appalachia over the native and highly esteemed pawpaw. Just like thimbleberries, pawpaws were once considered to have zero shelf life, "A wild treat, meant to be enjoyed in the wild," to borrow Cook's words. But veneration is high, nonetheless. So, Appalachian entrepreneurs figured out how to bring pawpaw flavor to the market in a variety of ways, first by creating an assortment of value-added foodstuffs. In southeastern Ohio, you can now find pawpaw fruit pops, ice cream, jams, and jellies in Kroger. One brewer makes a fruity lager with pawpaw, and a distiller finds the fruit's beguiling flavors of vanilla, banana, and mango perfect for suffusing his brandy.

Pawpaw orchardists and breeders witnessed the growing demand for pawpaw flavor and recently succeeded in developing larger fruit with comelier and thicker skin—traits grocers desire—while maintaining that heady tropical flavor that consumers desire. Meaning fresh pawpaws are now appearing at farmers markets for the masses to enjoy; no wilderness trekking required.

Lloyd says the thimbleberry is greatly underappreciated, and I concur. As an ardent fan of the thimbleberry, I hope folks in the PNW consider the burgeoning success in Appalachia with the pawpaw—and their own breeding success with the marionberry—and find ways to bring one of the region's finest flavors to a greater public.

BERRYBURG, USA

Alas, the Oregon Berry Festival is no more. The festival's first year was funded with grant money from the USDA's Specialty Crop program, and it then relied on private sponsorships the following years. Two years after the Berry Festival's commencement, Feast Portland was created, a multiday foodie extravaganza celebrating every comestible and cocktail under the PNW sun. Sponsorships became harder to source for the one-day berry festival while Feast Portland's popularity grew exponentially. Organizers decided to shutter the Oregon Berry Festival and, instead, participate in Feast Portland, albeit with a smaller presence.

Still, there are many reasons I consider Portland ground zero for berry exploration. First and foremost is the city's unique geography. Portland lies at the northern tip of the Willamette Valley, flanked by the Coast Ranges on the west and the Cascades on the east. Thanks to the foresight of Portland's city planners, the municipality established an urban growth boundary, limiting population sprawl and ensuring easy access to these wildernesses. Less than a fifty-minute drive from my hotel in the Pearl District I entered Tillamook State Forest, a beautifully rugged, sylvan patch of Oregon's Cascade Range. Here, red and evergreen huckleberries, salmonberries, thimbleberries, salal, Oregon grape, blackcaps (black raspberries), trailing blackberries, and wild strawberries abound. "Pick a trail, any trail," the ranger advised, which proved sound. I had easy access to a host of tasty, indigenous fruits.

The next day, I pointed my car east and drove straight at Mount Hood. In one hour, I was hiking in the Salmon-Huckleberry Wilderness, collecting buckets of black hucks and Cascade bilberries. In the peak of summer, it doesn't matter which direction you head from Portland; you will find wild berries by the bunches.

Another fortuitous result of good city planning for the berry curious is Portland's Forest Park. At over five thousand acres, Forest Park is one of the largest urban forests in the United States. Just five minutes into the park the din of urban density is silenced, and there were points along my trail that felt as remote as anywhere in the Tillamook State Forest or the Salmon-Huckleberry Wilderness. Here, salal, red huckleberry, blackberries, and thimbleberries (and those palate-puckering Oregon grapes) predominate. I literally gorged on a variety of bramble fruit one summer afternoon, they were so plentiful.

Alas, I found out later I dined illegally. I have to mention that official city policy prohibits the defacing of any public shrub or plant. Apparently, this includes picking berries. Jays can gorge all they want, but humans cannot taste a single fruit. *Sigh.* Still, for the berry newbie, there is great value in examining berry shrubs and vines of all types in their natural environs and to be able to confidently identify edible fruit before ingesting (including recognizing the foliage and habit of berry bushes even when no fruit is present). I consider urban forests such as Forest Park an excellent opportunity for such self-guided lessons.

Forest Park. It's easy to forget six hundred thousand people live just beyond these boughs.

If hiking isn't your thing, try foraging of a different sort and poke around Portland's bars, restaurants, and markets. No other city in the PNW utilizes berries in their dishes and drinks like Portlanders. At one bar, I found a marionberry whiskey, an incredibly smooth spirit from Portland's Eastside Distilling. This whiskey was more purple than the caramel color of most domestic whiskeys, especially noticeable when served in an unadorned rocks glass with one large rock—the ambient light refracts through the ice, accentuating the purple hue. I also found the marionberry flavor to be surprisingly pronounced; quite welcome and complementary to the woodsy flavors typical of whiskey. (It was exceptional when mixed with lemonade.)

You'll find the usual wild berry preserves in all the markets, but also something a bit unusual: berry salsa. This was everywhere! It's a fun, refreshing, place-based spin on a condiment that for forty-five years of my life I assumed had to have tomatoes. (Portlanders swap out tomatoes for fresh Oregon berries—

any berries. The jalapeño peppers, red onion, cilantro, and citrus juice often remain from traditional salsa recipes.)

Indeed, it doesn't matter where you venture in Portland— through a dense thicket of evergreens just outside of town or a dense stand of concrete buildings in the downtown, berries are ubiquitous.

BERRY RECIPES

The highlight of the Oregon Berry Festival was the gala dinner, held on the outdoor terrace of OMSI, the Oregon Museum of Science and Industry. Summer is generally quite comfortable in Portland, but the blistering 97°F temperature that day was an exception. With another three hours of daylight, it wasn't going to get comfortable anytime soon. In this sort of swelter, the food I find most appetizing is fresh, juicy, and fruity produce with invigorating acidity. Thankfully, this night's meal was all about berries.

Like most, when I think of berry dishes, I typically think of desserts or sweet additions to breakfast, like cereal, yogurt, pancakes, and smoothies. But Portlanders think about berries differently. I don't know if I needed even one hand to count the number of savory berry dishes I've tasted before my visit to Portland. But by the time we all sat down at our tables, we had already gorged on delectable hors d'oeuvres of blueberry empanada with ginger and green onion chimichurri, smoked pork with a raspberry glaze and herbed salsa, and salmon and spot prawns with herbs and marionberries wrapped in butter lettuce.

That meal at OMSI opened my eyes to the culinary versatility of the region's iconic fruits. I discovered cocktails, appetizers, and entrées (and desserts, of course) could all be enhanced when Oregon's native berries are prominent. I thought a fun and tasty way to illustrate my discovery was to include four recipes for an entire meal, from aperitif to dessert.

MARIONBERRY COCKTAIL

(Makes 4 cocktails)

Recipe courtesy of Eastside Distilling

As soon as the berry festival dinner guests arrived at OMSI and were escorted to the dining terrace, we rushed straight to the bar. All of us sought something cool and refreshing to drink to help cope with the searing heat still radiating from the pavement. Portland's own Eastside Distilling was on hand, mixing a variety of berry-inspired drinks from their assortment of locally distilled spirits. I opted for their marionberry cocktail, a spritely mix of fresh marionberry juice and fresh-squeezed lemons with white rum and a sprig of mint. That drink proved to be the perfect summer sipper and a beautiful way to showcase one of Oregon's beloved berries.

INGREDIENTS

1 pint fresh marionberries,
  juiced (see following)
4 lemons, juiced
White rum

Cacao syrup
Seltzer water
1 small bunch fresh mint, for
  garnish

PREPARATION

A few hours ahead, make the marionberry juice. Rinse one pint of fresh, ripe marionberries and place into a saucepan with just enough water to make the fruits bob. Bring to a boil slowly, then mash the berries with a potato masher in the water. Bring liquid back to a boil, then remove from heat.

Pour the berry mixture into a chinois and mash some more with a wooden dowel or the back of a wooden spoon, collecting all the juice into a bowl. Set juice in refrigerator to cool until happy hour. Meanwhile, squeeze the ripe lemons until 6 ounces of juice is obtained.

Add 1 jigger each of the marionberry juice, lemon juice, white rum, and cacao syrup into a shaker filled with ice. Shake lightly then strain into a highball glass and add a splash of seltzer water. Repeat for the remaining three cocktails. Garnish each drink with a sprig of mint, and have fun!

MARIONBERRY, SALMON, AND PRAWN LETTUCE CUPS

(Makes 15–20 hors d'oeuvres, depending on the number of lettuce leaves)

Recipe courtesy of Ryan Morgan, executive chef, Oregon Museum of Science and Industry

All the berry-themed dishes at the Oregon Berry Festival's Gala Dinner were gorgeous and sumptuous, but I found this appetizer the most intriguing. For one, it features two other native PNW flavors. It is also an incredibly light and healthy bite of food, yet fat on flavor; perfect for sizzling summer days. Mostly, I was amazed that blackberries and fish complemented each other so well. Never would I have thought to pair marionberries with prawns and salmon, but the combination with the fresh herbs and lemon juice was delightful.

INGREDIENTS

1 pound whole spot prawns
1 pound salmon lox
¼ teaspoon fresh tarragon,
   minced
¼ teaspoon fresh basil,
   minced
¼ teaspoon fresh cilantro,
   minced

1 teaspoon fish sauce
1 lemon, zested and juiced
Sea salt and freshly cracked
   pepper, to taste
1 head butter lettuce, leaves
   pulled apart
1 pint fresh marionberries

PREPARATION

Heat a large stock pot of water to a boil, and drop in the prawns—head, tail, vein, and all—and boil until just pink. Quickly remove the prawns from the pot and plunge them into a large bowl of ice water to halt the cooking. Once cooled, clean, peel, and devein the prawns and give them a rough chop. Place the meat into a large bowl and set aside.

Dice the cured salmon into a comparable size as the prawns, and add to the bowl. Now add the minced herbs, fish sauce, and a touch of the lemon juice and zest. Season with a little sea salt and fresh cracked pepper and mix thoroughly but gently. Taste the mixture and add more lemon juice, salt, or pepper if necessary. Once the seasonings are spot on, allow the mixture to sit for an hour, allowing the flavors to meld.

Spread the lettuce leaf cups onto a large platter and place a couple spoonfuls of the herbed fish mixture onto each leaf. Top the mixture with a plump Oregon marionberry and serve.

ROASTED DUCK AND BROCCOLINI WITH HUCKLEBERRY RELISH

(Makes 4 servings)

Recipe courtesy of Chef Jason Freeburg, Table FIVE 08

Driving back to California after the festival, I pulled into Salem for an early dinner. I looked up a few online reviews and found Table FIVE 08 highly recommended—a modern, hip eatery on bustling State Street in the downtown. I wasn't hankering for anything in particular, and I certainly didn't expect to find another savory berry dish.

But there it was: *Roasted duck and broccolini with spicy huckleberry relish.* No need for me to give the menu another thought, I knew exactly what I was ordering.

I thoroughly enjoyed every berry treat I tasted at the Oregon Berry Festival—savory as well as sweet. But this unexpected surprise in Salem was my hands-down favorite. As I admitted in the previous recipe, I was surprised fish and blackberries pair so well; but roasted duck with huckleberries blew my mind. When I returned home, I immediately contacted Chef Jason Freeburg and asked for the recipe, and he graciously obliged.

This recipe will work equally well with blueberries, but try to use black huckleberries if possible. They are easy to source if you're anywhere in the Pacific Northwest during the summer (including Idaho and Montana), or else through mail order.

INGREDIENTS

Duck and Broccolini

4 duck breasts with skin
2 pounds broccolini

Drizzle olive oil
Sea salt and pepper, to taste

Huckleberry Relish

2 pints black huckleberries
1 small bunch green onion, minced
2 tablespoons olive oil

2 tablespoons balsamic vinegar
¼ teaspoon chili flakes
Sea salt and pepper, to taste

PREPARATION

Duck and Broccolini

Begin by prepping the duck a day in advance, if possible. Pat each breast with a paper towel until dry, then score the skin with a very sharp knife in a cross-hatch pattern. (Be careful not to slice into the breast meat.) Place the breasts on a paper towel lined plate and refrigerate, uncovered, overnight. This will dry out the skin and ensure crispness.

Trim away one inch from the end of each broccolini stem, and then drop them all into a pot of boiling water for 90 seconds. Remove broccolini and immediately plunge into an ice bath to halt cooking. Drain and then set aside.

Preheat the oven to 400°F and heat a dry skillet over medium heat. Place the duck breasts skin-side down onto the hot skillet and sear until the skins are brown and crisp; about 6 to 8 minutes. Remove the breasts from the skillet and place on a baking sheet, skin-side up.

Place the blanched broccolini on another baking sheet and drizzle with olive oil, salt, and pepper. Place the duck and broccolini into the preheated oven to roast. After 5 minutes, remove the duck breasts and let rest for 2 to 3 minutes. The broccolini can continue to roast until the duck has been plated.

Huckleberry Relish

Huckleberries can be tender, and the vinegar used in the relish can break the skin and turn the pulp into mush. So it's best to prepare this dressing right before serving, while the duck is resting and the broccolini finishes roasting.

Place the huckleberries in a colander and rinse under cold water. Shake dry, then pour them into a large bowl. Add the minced green onion, olive oil, balsamic vinegar, chili flakes, and salt and pepper to taste. Gently toss the ingredients with your hands, then spoon the relish onto the side of a plate.

Slice each duck breast into 5 or 6 slices and place down the center of the plate alongside the relish. Finish the plating with the broccolini and serve immediately.

WILD OREGON BERRIES WITH LIMONCELLO CREAM

(Makes 8 servings)

This is a fantastic dessert to showcase the multitude of Oregon's wild berries. It is colorful, flavorful, and just plain fun.

There are two complementary flavors in this dish that really let these native PNW berries sing. One is the Italian cream cheese, mascarpone, which adds a luxurious mouthfeel and accentuates the berry flavors. The other is lemon. Pastry chefs know that lemon and berries are perfectly harmonious, and the Meyer lemon zest with the limoncello elevate a simple berry cup to a decadent adult treat.

If you love nuts, try sprinkling chopped hazelnuts (also known as filberts) onto the cream topping with the lemon zest. Oregon leads the nation in commercial hazelnut production, and one species, the western beaked hazelnut, is indigenous to the Pacific Northwest.

INGREDIENTS

¾ cup chilled whipping cream
½ cup mascarpone cheese
3 tablespoons white granulated
  sugar
3 tablespoons limoncello
3 cups thimbleberries
3 cups black huckleberries

1 cup salal
1 cup salmonberries
½ cup marionberry preserves
3 tablespoons Meyer lemon
  zest
Optional: ¼ cup hazelnuts,
  chopped

PREPARATION

Combine whipping cream, mascarpone, sugar, and limoncello in a medium bowl, and beat using an electric mixer until mixture becomes thick but is still creamy.

In a larger bowl, combine the fresh berries and preserves and one tablespoon of the lemon zest. Mix very gently using your fingers, as thimbleberries are quite delicate. Divide the berry mixture among 8 champagne coupes or ramekins. Top each serving with the limoncello-mascarpone cream then sprinkle with the additional lemon zest and, if desired, chopped hazelnuts.

6

Seattle:
KING OF KINGS

Troll-caught Chinook salmon, also known as king salmon.
Courtesy of Marcus Donner / www.marcusdonner.com

◇◇◇◇◇◇◇◇◇◇◇◇◇◇◇

Ask Seattleites to name an iconic food of their region (besides coffee), and they will not hesitate to answer. Salmon is more than just food in the Emerald City; it is intrinsic to Seattle's history and culture and remains perhaps the strongest bond with the region's First Peoples. Naturally, salmon is the meat of choice up here; it is to Seattleites what beef is to the other 320 million Americans. It is the prime cut, and the cornerstone of the city's cuisine.

Which is why I was heading up I-5 from Sacramento for a lunch in Seattle. You're probably thinking, "That better be some special salmon!" And it is. So special, few would recognize it as salmon even after they see it on their plate. But that's all about to change soon, and high time it does.

◇◇◇◇◇◇◇◇◇◇◇◇◇◇◇◇◇◇

I've become a huge fan of Slow Food over the years, especially their Ark of Taste. The Ark of Taste is an international catalog of regionally distinct heritage foods—those with superlative flavor, deep cultural traditions, or environmental significance. It is a database of flavors we should already have in the fore of our consciousness, yet, for one reason or another, have been largely forgotten. Slow Food's ethos is *Eat it to save it*, which may sound counterintuitive. But the Ark of Taste is a reminder of the unique breeds of cattle and sheep, fish, and heirloom varieties of fruits and vegetables that at one time were quite special in each of our corners of the world. If new generations discover the flavors our forefathers once revered, Slow Food believes we will work hard to preserve those species and varieties. And that logic has proved sound. The organization has been indispensable in helping maintain biodiversity of the animals and plants we use for food, ensuring healthier ecosystems and satisfied palates.

Perusing Slow Food's catalog of heritage foods, I came across a fish that was new to me: Washington Marbled Chinook. Chinook is one of five species of salmon native to the Pacific Northwest, along with Coho (Silver), Sockeye (Red), Pink (Humpback), and Keta (Chum or Dog). These five fishes are staples in the region's pantry. You might meet someone allegiant to Sockeye, or another who insists Coho is the most princely. But most chefs and diners would bequeath the crown to Chinook, the largest of the five species, the fattiest, and the least abundant. It is so prized in the Pacific Northwest that folks here often refer to it by another name: king salmon.

Fillet a king salmon and you will likely see the coral red flesh we all expect of this fish. But once in a great while, due to an anomaly in pigmentation, a Chinook will have ivory white flesh. And sometimes, if you cut open a Chinook, especially one caught in the Salish Sea, you see yet another variation: a softly mottled pink color, an intermixing of the typical coral red pigmentation with the rare white. This marbled salmon is special, and is the one listed on Slow Food's Ark of Taste.

The range of all Chinook is extensive, extending from San Francisco north to Alaska, along the Aleutian Islands and across the Bering Sea, down along the eastern Siberian coast and on to Hokkaido, Japan. But *marbled* Chinook occurs predominantly in the Washington and southwestern British Columbia fisheries. Biologists still don't understand the genetics behind it, but research to date shows that marbled Chinook are spawned in the tributaries of the lower Fraser River in British Columbia: the Harrison, Vedder, and Chilliwack Rivers. It is an unusually precise location, especially for a species with such a broad range, making marbled Chinook the only readily identifiable, regionally distinct salmon of *any* species, king or otherwise. This remarkable example of a place-specific food is why it was boarded onto the Ark of Taste.

Though this unique salmon made it onto Slow Food's list of legacy foods, marbled chinook lacks the sort of traditions, histories, and reverence we see tied to other heritage food animals. At the time of its induction into Slow Food's database, many fishermen didn't feel it was worth the effort to bring the fish from the boat to the dock. Once they discovered they had caught a marbled Chinook—which is only detectable once it has been killed and cut open as all Chinook have the same look to their scales and fins—it was flipped back into the water, dinner for any

Chinook salmon fillets on a bed of cedar boughs; marbled up front, red in back. *Courtesy of Amy Grondin*

nearby marine carnivores. Consumers, unaware another salmon option existed, wanted pure red Chinook. Fishmongers and chefs who play to consumer demand couldn't sell marbled salmon, so wholesalers and distributors didn't buy it, leaving the fishermen with little choice but to dump it. Twenty years ago, this regionally distinct fish, exalted by the eco-minded epicures of Slow Food, was considered garbage simply because it looked different.

CHAMPIONS OF THE MARGINALIZED

I became fascinated with marbled Chinook, but outside of a couple of articles and what was noted on Slow Food's website, I couldn't find much information about it. After a bit of digging, I came across a champion of this lowly king, one of the fishermen who was responsible for getting marbled Chinook aboard the ark. I had to meet this person, to learn more about this unique salmon and that special lunch I wanted to attend in Seattle.

I met Amy Grondin at a café in her hometown of Port Townsend, a picturesque community on the Olympic Peninsula about an hour east of Port Angeles. I ordered my usual espresso macchiato, she got her coffee, and then she introduced me to another fisherman from the area. Joel Kawahara is a quiet, congenial, extremely modest and immediately likable man, so different from the stereotypically loud, salty, boastful fisherman I have always harbored in my mind. I was quickly impressed with Kawahara's encyclopedic knowledge of salmon. Just a few minutes into our conversation, he was explaining the intricacies of salmon fishing, how to tell where they will be swimming based on the temperature of the sea, and what they would be eating at any given time of the year.

Amy and her husband, Greg, own and fish from F/V *Duna*, and Joel's boat is F/V *Karolee*, fishing vessels specifically equipped for trolling. Trolling is a method of selective fishing that catches one fish at a time by towing leaders with baited hooks through the water. It is very different from the similar sounding trawling, which drags large nets behind the boat, indiscriminately ensnaring entire schools of fish. Trawling can be quite harmful to the marine environment, especially when those nets are dragged along the ocean floor, wrecking sensitive habitat.

Trawling also traps species of fish that aren't intended to be caught. This is called *bycatch*, a term most Americans became familiar with in the late 1980s when dolphin-safe tuna hit the supermarket shelves. Trolling, on the other hand, is quite benign to the environment, and bycatch is virtually eliminated. There can only be one fish on each hook, and it is baited with food or lures that are particularly attractive to the targeted fish. Even if a nontargeted fish takes the bait, as they sometimes do, trollers simply release it from the hook and let it swim away.

Trolling also results in some of the highest quality fish. Because each fish is handled one at a time, there is minimal bruising and scale loss that typically result when entire schools of thrashing fish are scooped out of the sea. Troll-caught fish are bled and cleaned immediately after they are landed, which ensures appealing firmness and good flavor. With some netting methods, many fish die before they are even lifted out of the water. The longer the blood and viscera remain in a dead fish, the worse the texture and flavor will be.

We then got onto the subject of freshness. I know some trolling boats stay out at sea for days at a time before heading back to the docks to sell their catch. If salmon were caught two days prior—even if it is fresh and packed on ice—wouldn't that compromise flavor? "You don't want to eat a *fresh* fresh salmon," Kawahara said, "as in 'just-killed' fresh." This caught me by surprise. I thought fresh fish was, "Hey, look what I just caught, let's eat it!" But Joel explained that shortly after death, the muscles stiffen tightly; rigor mortis. Salmon meat during this initial stage of decomposition is of poor texture and flavor. It takes days for the muscles to relax and become pliable again. "The best tasting salmon is about three days dead," Joel said. Which got me thinking. "How long has the fresh salmon in the grocery store been dead?" Amy and Joel said it depends on the supply chain, but the common route of fisherman-wholesaler-distributor-fishmonger / restaurant / supermarket takes about a week or longer. Reason alone to connect with your local fisherman and buy more directly.

As the conversation moved to marbled Chinook and Slow Food, I asked Amy, "Why champion a fish that consumers don't find appealing? More to the point, why *don't* they find it appealing?" Her answer was straightforward: consumers expect salmon to be red. Any salmon that is not that familiar salmon color, even if it is fresh and firm and exhibits an appetizing mottled pink hue, must be inferior, we think. "If we could pull a king salmon out of the water, readily identify it as red, white, or marbled, and return the less valuable, non-red specimens safely back to the sea, it wouldn't be much of a concern," Amy said. "The

Greg Grondin landing a gorgeous Chinook salmon on the F/V Duna. *Courtesy of Amy Grondin*

problem is, regardless of flesh color all Chinook have the same exterior appearance so we can't tell them apart from glance and return it to the sea, alive." That's when Joel and Amy described a disturbingly unethical, highly illegal practice that had been growing rampant among the salmon fisherman in the area.

High grading is the commercial harvesting of large quantities of product—like timber or minerals or fish—and keeping only the best and most marketable goods, discarding the rest. It is an environmentally destructive practice, especially deplorable in Chinook fishing, as the value of the goods aren't tied to the vigor or quality of the fish, rather the whim of a trend that prizes one flesh color over another. Such is the case with marbled Chinook.

Red, white, and marbled Chinook are all the same species of fish, *Oncorhynchus tshawytscha*. The outward appearance of marbled Chinook is the same as any other Chinook—a bluish-green back speckled with black spots, bright silver flanks, a white belly and iridescent tail, black lips and gums. But as I mentioned, only once the fish is landed and cut open will the fisherman know the color of its meat.

Fishermen like Kawahara and Grondin know that marbled Chinook is delicious, and has a distinctive flavor, on par with (some say even better than) the red-fleshed kings. Some cooks know it, too; but consumers do not. So, imagine this: You're a salmon fisherman. Chinook is the largest of the Pacific salmonids and has the highest fat content, so it consequently fetches the best prices—about thirty-five dollars a pound at retail. But some years, for whatever reason, almost half of your Chinook catch is marbled, and the most you can get for this fish is thirty-five *cents* a pound; one-tenth the value of a typical Chinook. To ensure sustainability, the Washington Department of Fish and Game sets a limit on how many salmon you can remove from the sea to sell. What do you do? If you're unscrupulous, you throw all the marbled Chinook (which are now dead) back into the water, rebait your hooks, and hope to catch some high-value red Chinook. It is a waste of delicious, nutritious food and puts the health of fish stocks in peril.

Some Washington troll fishermen had a different strategy. "What if we could prove to wholesalers and distributors, fishmongers and chefs, that marbled Chinook is every bit as unctuous and flavorful as a red king?" they thought. "What if we marketed the marbled salmon as 'The Fisherman's Favorite,' because we know just how special these fish are? There would be little reason to high grade Chinook if all of them commanded a good price." Grondin had found her calling.

It has been almost two decades of tireless championing by Grondin and a handful of her colleagues, and the efforts are paying off. The annual Washington Chinook Troll Salmon luncheon in Seattle that Grondin coordinates with the Coastal Trollers Association and the Makah Tribe was first held in 2004. Each year the event grows more popular, attracting a diversity of fishermen and distributors, culinary journalists, Fish and Game staff, ecologists and wild food advocates, as well as intrigued epicures. In 2006, she collaborated with Jeremy Brown of the Coastal Trollers Association and Gerry Warren, Slow Food's PNW regional governor, and the trio successfully boarded marbled Chinook onto the Ark of Taste. In 2008, the *Seattle Times* ran an article with the headline "Marbled salmon may be the next 'it' fish."

Marbled Chinook still doesn't fetch the same price as red, but the gap has closed considerably. "It's been a tremendous success in terms of increased awareness and publicity and ex-vessel price," Grondin says. Still, she recognizes the advocacy must continue. Despite the wider public acceptance of marbled Chinook, "Distributors are still selling it as a second-value fish."

One strategy Grondin employs when direct-marketing her catch is to ask the same price for all her king salmon, regardless if they are red, white, or marbled. "Fishermen might agree that marbled Chinook are worth every penny as red," she said, "but if you end up selling that fish at a reduced price, you've just convinced the buyer—and yourself—that marbled Chinook isn't as valuable." Grondin says she sells quality and flavor, not color:

> A chef purchases from me because the fish Greg and I produce are high quality. Our fish are fresh and sustainably caught, completely flushed of blood, chilled immediately and handled carefully to assure minimal scale loss. I do everything in my power to preserve the incredible texture and flavor inherent in salmon. All my fish are caught and handled with the same care regardless of flesh color. Because the condition of my fish is among the best, they all deserve delicacy pricing.

Amy has become a respected voice of sustainable fishing in Washington. When we last spoke, she broke the exciting news. "I've been invited to be part of a James Beard sponsored sustainable seafood panel at South by Southwest! Can you believe that? Me, a fisherman!" She was overjoyed, and rightfully so. She sighed and said, "You know, so many good things that have happened in my life happened because of salmon."

To which I would respond, and so many good things that have happened to marbled salmon's image have happened because of Amy.

MARBLED AND MARVELOUS

Grondin and Kawahara have probably eaten more marbled Chinook than anyone, and both agree the flavor is distinct, and deliciously so. I asked them how it differs from red, but they first clarified that the flavor of any salmon, king or Coho, red or white, changes because of numerous variables. For instance, changes in the salmons' diet as the season progresses affect flavor. In May, king salmon off the coast of Washington eat mostly small crustaceans, like krill and shrimp. So, salmon flavor in the spring tends to be milder. Later in the year, salmon consume forage fish with much more oil content and the flavor deepens. Mature salmon have more fat than younger fish, so their meat is more unctuous. Then there's *merroir*, an oft-used wordplay on the French *terroir* to describe the distinct flavor of fish caught from specific waters. Flavor also changes rapidly when a salmon has reached the end of its life cycle and is returning to the freshwater rivers and streams where it was born to spawn the next generation. Once a salmon sniffs freshwater, it stops feeding and begins to live off the fat that it has been storing while in salt water. If you can catch such a fish early in its journey back home, it will be full of fat. But catch that salmon in freshwater close to its spawning beds, after it has swum hundreds of miles from the open sea, and is battered and haggard and starved, and you will taste something quite inferior.

Holding diet, season, age, and locale constant, Grondin says marbled Chinook tastes lighter, more delicate, and a touch sweeter than the typical red. She used the flavor of crab and shrimp as a comparison. "Not quite as sweet as those shellfish," she clarified, "but certainly the marbled salmon has a seafood sweetness that isn't readily tasted in red Chinook."

I concocted a taste test, though I realize there were too many of those variables at play that Grondin and Kawahara had mentioned for this to be anything other than a fun experiment for my dinner guests and me. I purchased six-ounce portions of red, white, and marbled Chinook from a wild seafood purveyor in Bellingham, Washington. There was no way of knowing if these three fish were the same age or caught in the same waters, but I was told they were all local and all troll caught. I seasoned them the same and grilled them the same. I then served them to my esteemed dinner guests (Mom and Dad) for a side-by-side comparison.

Each of us found the three fillets mild and delicious. I would say the red Chinook had the strongest flavor, but not by much. The marbled Chinook had the firmest texture, however, which

Three salmon fillets, all Chinook: red, marbled, white.

was perfect for the grill. But all three were marvelous pieces of fish, rich and luscious, with the only seasonings being a splash of olive oil and sea salt. Nothing else was needed to enhance the flavor of these beautiful fillets. In the end, none of us could say with any conviction that the red Chinook tasted better than the marbled king or even the white.

Which is exactly what Grondin has been trying to tell us for the past two decades.

BITTER / RAW, SUSTAINABLE / DELICIOUS

I pulled off I-5 in Seattle, found Lark restaurant along the southern edge of the hip Capitol Hill neighborhood, and immediately went upstairs where Chef Johnathan Sundstrom recently expanded his space. Bitter / Raw is his shellfish and charcuterie bar perched on the mezzanine, and the new venue for the annual Washington Troll Salmon luncheon. While everyone is anxious to see what this James Beard winner had prepared this year, the principal reason we had gathered here is to acknowledge the environmental importance of sustainable fishing and to celebrate a heritage fish. For folks like me keen on great food and interested in how it gets to my plate, these lunches provide a rare opportunity to meet the fishermen, environmentalists, journalists, and purveyors—folks dedicated to delivering the best quality and flavor—together under one roof.

I met members from the Makah Tribe, the native peoples of the Olympic Peninsula and cosponsors of the annual lunch. These people taught fishermen like Grondin and Kawahara the old ways of catching salmon, which, as we have come to learn from all tribal customs and practices, creates harmony between us and Mother Nature. I also meet folks from the other cosponsoring organizations: Cape Flattery Fisherman's Cooperative (the commercial fishing operation of the Makah Tribe) and the Coastal Trollers Association. Amy and I chatted a bit and then she introduced me to Sarah Fisken, a representative of Washington Sea Grant, which is an educational extension of the University of Washington that works with fishermen, tribes, schools, government, and other organizations to offer research and funding to help improve marine ecosystems. Each of these experts shared insight with the myriad publishers and journalists in attendance, insights that would then be shared with the larger public through their respective magazines and newsletters. While eating, I overheard trollers boast of the wonderful flavor of their wild caught fish, each confirming the inferiority of farmed salmon. Pinot noir and chardonnay from Chinook Winery was flowing, and with every sip, the discussions got more passionate and provocative. This luncheon was truly a complete meal; a delicious affair that educated, inspired, and delighted.

Of course, the highlight of the afternoon was Chef John Sundstrom's dish. Each year the chef prepares something different. And each year he seems to outdo himself. For the eleventh annual luncheon in 2014, Chef Sundstrom served marbled Chinook with bright yellow kale blossoms and green chickpeas, diced Jamón serrano, and a parsley purée. It looked like a painting and was easily one of the prettiest seafood dishes I've ever witnessed. Another year, he kicked off the luncheon with a scrumptious tribute to Wolfgang Puck and his signature pizzas: a crust topped with smoked wild Chinook, crème fraiche, herbs, and ikura. He followed that appetizer with marbled Chinook, Parmigianino risotto espuma, bacon, morels, and spring onion. This year, Joel graciously donated a couple beautiful Chinooks, and Chef Sundstrom nestled each perfectly seared salmon fillet over a roasted beet purée, topping the dish with a porcini and duck fat buckwheat crumble.

During lunch, Amy got up to thank everyone in attendance and to share a few insights of her own. She invited me up to the front and we chatted about marbled Chinook and my enthusiasm for Pacific Northwest foods in general. Then a fisherman

The author and Amy Grondin share a few laughs with the crowd at the thirteenth annual Washington Troll Salmon luncheon.
Courtesy of Marcus Donner / www.marcusdonner.com

raised his hand, and he asked me how I prefer to cook Chinook. I responded without hesitation: "Grilled." This was fun, because it incited a boisterous reaction from the other guests. Obviously, everyone has their own opinion on the best way to cook such a special fish. Some agreed with me, but a few other fishermen insisted the traditional method was best, smoked with the sweet perfume of alder. One thought a simple poach was the proper way to truly to showcase pure Chinook flavor. Maxime Bilet, the coauthor of *Modernist Cuisine: The Art and Science of Cooking*, disagreed, and claimed sous vide is the only way to ensure perfect temperature, texture, and flavor.

But in the end, we were in Chef Sundstrom's house. After devouring his gorgeous fillet with the perfectly crisped skin and the melt-in-our-mouth texture still fresh on our tongues, we all agreed, he had the final word: pan-seared, skin-side down in a hot skillet, flipped then finished in a 400°F oven while the skin is lightly basted with melted butter.

MARBLED CHINOOK RECIPES

Ask a chef, a fisherman, and a food writer how to cook salmon, and you will hear three different answers. Which is largely why salmon is so highly revered; it's incredibly versatile and delicious, no matter how it is prepared.

Each of these recipes uses marbled Chinook; please seek it out (or else demand marbled Chinook from your local salmon purveyor). But any Chinook—red, white, or marbled—will work fabulously. Just insist it is fresh, wild, and troll caught.

Here we have three different preparations: Chef John Sundstrom's favorite method, Amy Grondin's, and mine.

PAN ROASTED MARBLED CHINOOK WITH SUGAR SNAP PEAS, RADISH, AND MORELS

(Makes 4 servings)

Recipe courtesy of Chef Johnathan Sundstrom, Lark

Chef Johnathan Sundstrom is a James Beard award winner for obvious reason. His style of cooking is eclectic but executed with remarkable talent. One meal might be a pure expression of Pacific Northwest cuisine, the next a delicious riff on California pizza (using PNW ingredients, of course), while another shows off his classical training in Japanese cuisine and sushi.

The annual Washington Troll Salmon luncheons held at Chef Sundstrom's restaurant are exquisite, and a fantastic opportunity for diners to witness John's command of so many different ingredients and cuisines. John's accompaniments and styles are ever evolving, but the way he cooks salmon fillets is often the same, which is easy to understand once you taste them. The skin is perfectly crisped, and the meat is unimaginably tender and moist. So, don't think of this recipe as a complete, must-try meal (even though it is). Think of this as a tutorial on the right way to sear a gorgeous, skin-on, Chinook salmon fillet.

INGREDIENTS

Butter Sauce

1 cup dry white wine
1 shallot, peeled and sliced
1 bay leaf
8 whole peppercorns
6 ounces butter, cold
Sea salt, to taste

Vegetables

2 tablespoons butter
½ cup morel mushrooms, cleaned and sliced
½ pound sugar snap peas
1 bunch French breakfast radishes, washed and quartered
1 tablespoon chives, sliced thin
Sea salt and fresh ground black pepper, to taste

Salmon

1 teaspoon olive oil
4 wild-caught, marbled Chinook
   fillets, about 4 to 6 ounces
   each, skin on (but scaled)

1 tablespoon butter
Sea salt and fresh ground
   black pepper, to taste

PREPARATION

Butter Sauce

Simmer the wine, shallot, bay leaf, and peppercorns until the liquid is reduced by ⅔. Whisk the cold butter into the wine a bit at a time, then strain the sauce through a fine mesh sieve. Season with salt, and reserve the sauce in a warm (but not hot!) part of the kitchen until ready to use.

Vegetables

Melt 1 tablespoon of the butter in a large sauté pan over medium heat and sauté the morels until caramelized. Meanwhile, blanch the sugar snap peas in salted, boiling water until just tender, remove and immediately plunge into an ice-water bath to halt the cooking. Do the same with the radishes. Drain the peas, slice in half, and set aside. Drain the radishes as well.

Add the peas, radishes, and the remaining tablespoon of butter to the sauté pan with the mushrooms. Reduce heat to low and warm gently. Add the chives and season with salt and pepper.

SALMON

Heat the oil in a large sauté pan over medium-high heat. Add the salmon fillets—skin-side down—and sear until the skins are golden and crispy. Drain the excess oil from the pan, then turn the fillets over (skin-side up) and place the entire pan in a 400°F oven.

Add the butter, and as it melts, baste the top of the salmon carefully. Cook until the salmon is medium rare to medium (probably no longer than 4 minutes). Remove the fillets from the pan, season with salt and pepper, and let rest 2 minutes before plating.

Spoon the warm vegetables into serving bowls, top with the cooked salmon fillets, and ladle the butter sauce around the salmon.

DUNA CHOWDER

(Makes 12 hungry fishermen-size servings)

Red Chinook on the left, marbled on the right.
Recipe courtesy of Amy Grondin, F/V Duna. *Photo Courtesy of Marcus Donner / www.marcusdonner.com*

Amy Grondin has eaten a lot of salmon and has tasted every culinary preparation from sashimi to sous vide. But this chowder, which is Grondin's creation, is special. Of course, the flavors are extraordinary, confirmation of the superior quality of fresh, troll-caught Chinook. And it is the perfect comfort food for old salts and fishermen alike (made especially tasty with the dose of umami contributed by wakame).

The dish is delicious. But one of my favorite parts of her chowder recipe is the preparation . . . something I rarely say. There is something sublime about cubes of red Chinook nestled against cubes of marbled salmon, lightly adorned with sea salt and a sprinkling of black pepper. I almost didn't want to cook the fish at all, it looked so tantalizing raw, just sitting there on the cutting board.

This is more than a simple fish chowder to Amy Grondin. This dish, named after her boat, F/V *Duna*, is dear because it was the meal she shared with fellow captains during a rainy day at sea; a delicious, hot, spirit-lifting bowl of soup that sparked an auspicious start to the summer fishing season. This meal gives Amy a deserved sense of pride, because it is, as she put it, "the recipe that fed the crews from five fishing boats."

INGREDIENTS

½ cup bacon, chopped
3½ cups onion, diced
1¾ cups celery, diced
2 tablespoons garlic, minced
4 bay leaves
2 teaspoons dill (dry is fine)
2 teaspoons thyme (dry is fine)
2 cups carrots, cut into ½ inch pieces
3–4 quarts fish stock
3–4 cups red skin potatoes or other thin-skinned spud, cut into 1-inch pieces
1 can corn, drained
1 pint heavy cream or 2 cans evaporated milk
3–4 pounds marbled Chinook (or red Chinook, or even both!), skinned and cut into 1-inch cubes
¼ cup dried wakame, crushed into small pieces
Salt and pepper to taste

PREPARATION

In a large stockpot over medium heat, sauté the bacon until the fat is rendered but the meat is not too crispy. Add the onion and celery, stirring occasionally until the vegetables are just soft, about 5 minutes.

Add the garlic, bay leaves, dill, and thyme, and sauté until fragrant, about 1 minute. Now add the carrots and fish stock, simmering until the carrots soften slightly. Scrape the bottom of the pot occasionally to loosen any bacon or vegetable bits.

Next add the potatoes, corn, and cream (or evaporated milk) and continue to simmer until the spuds are just slightly soft. Remember, keep stirring so nothing sticks to the bottom of the pot.

Once the potatoes are soft, adjust the heat to keep the broth steaming hot but below a boil. Now add the cubes of salmon and dried wakame. Give the chowder a gentle yet complete stir to submerge the fish and distribute the wakame throughout. Simmer until the fish is barely cooked throughout (check at 5 minutes). Remember the fish will continue to cook in the hot broth even when the pot is off the stove, so be careful not to overcook the fish or it will be chewy.

Season the soup with salt and pepper and ladle into large bowls. Serve with lots of warm bread, cold beer, and call it dinner.

Fisherman's Tip: Amy says, "You can make this chowder a day ahead if you wish. Stop just before you add the fish then cool and refrigerate the chowder. One hour before you wish to serve the chowder, gently heat the soup back up to a steamy simmer and add the raw fish and dried seaweed. Follow the recipe from that point onward."

GRILLED MARBLED CHINOOK AND SUMMER VEGETABLES

(Makes 4 servings)

When the weather turns warm and I begin to crave outdoor meals, nothing beats a beautiful cut of salmon lightly seasoned and quickly grilled. But now I grill my salmon differently. I used to only grill salmon steaks. If I grilled fillets, I started flesh-side down on the hot grill (skin up). But after talking with Chef Sundstrom (and tasting his amazing salmon twice now), I've changed how I grill salmon. I forgo steaks and always choose skin-on fillets, and I start skin-side down, so that I can get a deliciously charred, crispy skin while the flesh cooks more quietly and evenly. I flip the fillets during the last minute of cooking to get those grill marks we all love to see, which seem even more fetching against the pale pink flesh of marbled Chinook.

I find this dish easy to prepare because it cooks so quickly. The vegetables and the salmon can be cooked at the same time on the grill. If you have a small grill, or are cooking for more people, grill the vegetables first, then place them in a warm oven. You can then devote your full attention to grilling your fresh, wild-caught fish to perfection.

The sauce is a fun riff on a traditional tzatziki, which I find quite refreshing on hot days. Instead of cucumbers, I use shallots and ginger—two bold flavors that pair well with salmon—and then give it a wee bit of kick with chipotle chili flakes. But feel free to season as you wish, or even make a true tzatziki if that's what you prefer.

INGREDIENTS

Yogurt Sauce

1 tablespoon avocado oil (or any neutral flavored oil with a high smoke point)
1 medium shallot, minced
1 tablespoon pickled ginger, minced
2 cloves garlic, pressed
½ teaspoon chipotle chili flake
1 small Meyer lemon, juiced
1 ounce white wine (I like sauvignon blanc because I find the bright, citrusy zing pairs best with grilled fish and vegetables)
1 tablespoon fresh dill fronds (stems removed), minced
½ teaspoon sea salt (more or less, depending on your taste)
8 ounces Greek yogurt, plain

Summer Vegetables

4 medium sized zucchini, sliced lengthwise, ¼-inch thick
4 medium Ping Tung eggplant, sliced lengthwise, ¼-inch thick
¼ cup olive oil
Splash of white wine or lemon juice (to prevent eggplant from oxidizing)
½ teaspoon each salt and pepper (more or less, depending on your liking)

Salmon

4 wild-caught, marbled Chinook fillets, about 4 to 6 ounces each, skin on (but scaled)
Avocado oil
White pepper
Sea salt
Extra virgin olive oil

PREPARATION

Yogurt Sauce

I recommend making the yogurt sauce well in advance. This allows the flavors to meld and frees up your time so you can give full attention to the salmon and veggies, which cook in just a few minutes.

In a small saucepan, heat the oil over a medium-low flame. Add the shallots and sauté until translucent. Add the pickled ginger, garlic, chili flakes, lemon juice, and white wine and continue to cook until the liquid is reduced by half.

Place the dill and salt in a medium mixing bowl and then pour the shallot-ginger-garlic sauce over the herbs and mix well. Now add the yogurt and blend completely. (If you prefer a smoother sauce, throw everything into a food processor.)

Chill the yogurt sauce for at least 2 hours to let the flavors meld.

Summer Vegetables

Place the sliced zucchini and eggplant in a large salad bowl, and add the olive oil, wine (or lemon juice), salt, and pepper. Using your fingers, gently toss until each slice is thoroughly coated. Set aside while you prepare the salmon for grilling.

Salmon

Begin by removing any pin bones from each fillet with tweezers. Be thorough but gentle. Ripping pin bones from the flesh destroys the texture of the meat.

Brush each fillet with avocado oil and then season with a sprinkling of white pepper and salt. I prefer to go light on the seasonings so you can better taste the pure flavor of marbled Chinook. Now it's time to prepare the grill.

Grilling

Since the vegetables and salmon cook very quickly, temperature modulation is imperative. It is easy to overcook salmon and delicate vegetables like eggplant and zucchini. For these reasons, I prefer to use a 3-burner gas grill so I have quick, direct control over the heat across the grate surface.

Begin with a clean, well-oiled grill grate. Turn all 3 burners to high, close the lid, and heat to 450–500°F. Once the grill is preheated, turn off the center burner and place your salmon fillets—skin-side down!—in the middle of the grill. This method employs the best of direct and indirect grilling. The grate is so hot it will sufficiently sear and crisp the salmon skin. But since the center burner is off, you reduce the risk of overcooking the salmon.

Turn the left and right burners down to about medium. Place the eggplant slices in a single layer on one side of the salmon fillets, and the zucchini on the other. Close the grill lid and sear the veggies about 2 minutes until those tantalizing char markings are clearly evident, then flip each slice. Continue to cook until vegetables are just tender. Remove and place on a platter.

At this point, the salmon should be close to done. Flip the fillets and sear until light grill markings appear. Remove the salmon. The fish will continue to cook even off the grill, so make sure you remove the salmon from the grill when the meat is almost—but not quite—completely done. The old adage "cook until the flesh easily flakes with a fork" is too long! You want to remove the fish when the sections of flesh begin to pull apart, but do not quite flake. Brush the finished salmon with a little bit of your favorite extra virgin olive oil.

To serve, grab a spoon and ladle enough yogurt sauce to swipe a generous smear across the plate. Layer a few slices of eggplant and zucchini atop the yogurt, then finish plating with the grilled salmon.

7

Lummi Island:
HYPERLOCAL

Sunset over the San Juan Islands.

◇◇◇◇◇◇◇◇◇◇◇◇◇◇◇◇◇◇

Way up in the northwestern reaches of the continental United States—further north than even Victoria, British Columbia—there is a really special restaurant in a really special place. Here, on the shores of a remote island whose name rhymes with "yummy," American cuisine is being redefined.

But you'll have to work a bit if you wish to witness this culinary evolution firsthand. I hopped a plane to Seattle, picked up a rental car, and drove two hours north on I-5, following the curvilinear shoreline along Puget Sound. Fifteen miles before I hit Canada, I did a buttonhook around Bellingham Bay, drove south through a tribal reservation, then hit a dead end. I was at the edge of the American mainland, looking out to my destination over a narrow channel, not even a mile across. Yet there wasn't a bridge, only a ferry—and I had just missed it.

It would be forty minutes before the *Whatcom Chief* departed the mainland again—the only public access to Lummi Island. That gave me enough time to stretch my legs and survey my surroundings. I flew over this patch of the country once when I took a puddle jumper from Seattle to Vancouver. I have traveled extensively through the United States and consider my knowledge of American geography quite strong. But this had not looked like any landscape I had ever seen before, domestic or foreign. There were so many islands—Orcas, Lopez, San Juan, Guemes, Lummi; mountainous forms blanketed by evergreen trees and encircled by royal blue straits named Rosario and Haro. It seemed paradisiacal! Now, standing in a spot I had flown over just a few years earlier, the landscape didn't look any less exotic.

I had found my ignorance of this stunning landscape was shared among many of my compatriots. I boasted about my "discovery" of such a beautiful land, tucked away in the upper-left corner of our country. Few others had even heard of this geographical treasure, much less visited—including a great many West Coasters. But as I said, that was a few years ago. Today, those sylvan islands have appeared on most every epicure's radar—as a bucket list travel destination—thanks to a young man in an old house.

WELCOME TO THE WILLOWS INN

Any gastronome interested in American eateries undoubtedly knows Chef Blaine Wetzel's story: a kid from Olympia who started cooking at a steakhouse in a Walmart parking lot at the age of fourteen before going to culinary school in Scottsdale, Arizona. From there, Wetzel honed his craft at top notch restaurants from Las Vegas to Carmel, California, and eventually on to Copenhagen, where he did a two-year stint at Noma under René Redzepi, who was considered the world's best chef at the time (and still is, by many accounts). It was here that Wetzel caught Redzepi's passion for creating new, exciting dishes using wild, native ingredients.

Homesick for Puget Sound, Wetzel answered a Craigslist ad for a chef to take over the kitchen at a century-old inn on a scarcely populated island in the Salish Sea. He may have thought he was running away from the frantic rat race of culinary celebrity. When Blaine answered that Craigslist ad, he really wanted to get back home and work an easy job, as he put it, until he figured out what to do next. As it turned out, Blaine ran headlong into his dream.

That was 2010, and the next chapter of Blaine's story tells how he can pluck every species of fish, grass, tree, bulb, flower, and weed from Lummi Island and turn out the most sublime, sumptuous dishes. The epicurean glossies and the restaurant reviews tell the tale of how a bed-and-breakfast that for nine-tenths of its one-hundred-year history had served mediocre fare at best became one of the most exciting restaurants in the world—seemingly overnight!—because of the resourcefulness and confidence and creativity of the new chef in town. As the articles about Blaine Wetzel and The Willows Inn accumulated, so did the accolades: *Food & Wine* Best New Chef 2012, James Beard Rising Star Chef of the Year 2014, and James Beard again, this time anointing Blaine Best Chef in the Northwest 2015.

Cooking with whatever fruit or fish or fungus Lummi Island produces isn't some culinary conceit from a gifted and confident chef. In fact, nothing could be further from the truth. The reality is, cooking with the Lummi Island provender is a necessity.

If you recall my planes, automobiles, and ferries experience, the island is remote. It is extremely difficult to procure fresh and varied ingredients from other regions; it's simply cost prohibitive. Fortunately, Wetzel can stock the largest of pantries with whatever grows in and around the island, making the ecosystem seem like an obvious gastronomic luxury. But it's a luxury that isn't obvious to other, equally talented chefs.

Wetzel recalls when he first arrived on Lummi Island, it took some time to find his voice as a chef. While the landscape inspired Blaine, he admitted it was also overwhelming. "It takes a while to connect with your natural surroundings, follow their rhythms, and know what to serve when," he explains, in his provocative, lavishly illustrated book *Sea and Smoke*. "Working at The Willows was my first opportunity to respond to the most spectacular and diverse ingredients I had ever seen."

Once he found his voice, Wetzel soon was confidently marrying produce from the farm down the road with the island's indigenous fare, and in the process, creating combinations of

Dungeness crab in a purée of pine nuts—one of the twenty courses I had during an unforgettable meal at The Willows.

flavors and textures with American ingredients few Americans have heard of before, including longtime Pacific Northwesterners. Pumpkin seeds and candied angelica; turnip stems and caramelized razor clam; salmonberries and beach roses; wild nettles and crispy mustard leaves; these are just a few of the dishes from my meal served on May 9, 2016. Blaine's food is a celebration of native flavors, with each tiny dish heralding a singular ingredient from the island. I don't think of his menu as a multicourse meal, but as a collection of *amuse-bouches*, a delightful list of hearty bites straight outta the PNW. Clearly, this is not your typical restaurant fare. But never has a region's diverse, indigenous flavors been presented so purely—and expertly.

The dinner I had that spring evening at The Willows was my epiphany meal (I think every epicure has one). Of course, I'm a huge fan and advocate of America's native produce, because I know it can be delicious. I just didn't realize it could be *this* delicious, and speak so clearly to the region. The focused, place-based flavor that defines Wetzel's cuisine surprises every diner, even the most seasoned chefs and critics. Kevin Pang of the *Chicago Tribune* penned one of the restaurant's first reviews back in 2011, just one year after Wetzel arrived (when the chef was still searching for his culinary voice, undoubtedly). Pang wrote:

> The realization comes that this dinner could only exist here and now. In the finest restaurants in the world—Per Se, Alinea, The French Laundry—there's nothing New York, Chicago or Bay Area about those places. The Willows Inn has what the French call terroir: It is symbiotically connected with Lummi Island. Nowhere else could this food exist, in no other time can this menu take place.

Blaine brushes off any compliment touting his astounding ability. He clarified—to me and to his readers—the basis of his

Slices of geoduck; simple, sublime.

cuisine isn't so much about technique but rather about "incredible ingredients that speak to you." He acknowledges that many diners find these ingredients unusual, even exotic. After all, many are ones his patrons have never read on a menu before. "But they're not exotic in that they're expensive and rare," Wetzel says, "just hyperlocal."

SPEAKING FOR THE TREES

Pulling into The Willows Inn, up the short, gravel incline, guests catch an unobstructed view of what might be the most enchanting piece of the property. The backyard is quite rustic—a clearing in a thicket of alder and cedar and pine and fir, with a few boulders and smoothly weathered, sculpturesque tree trunks scattered about. Pyramids of firewood are stacked all around, and a wooden picnic table sits in the clearing, often empty, but occasionally hosting one of the kitchen staff as they wolf down a quick meal. But the focal point of the yard is a modestly sized, limestone-clad, woodfired grill and the tall, tin-roofed shack emanating white plumes of sweet smoke. It is over that searing grill and in that perfumed smokehouse that Blaine performs some of his best magic.

"A simple smoked mussel," was the very first dish Wetzel served Grant Achatz, the freakishly creative, astoundingly talented chef at Alinea. "That is all it was. And all of what it was," Chef Achatz wrote, in his foreword to *Sea and Smoke*. At the time, Wetzel was just twenty-six, but his youth belied his capacity. "Sincere, provocative, mature, and intelligent," Achatz wrote, describing the voice of Wetzel's cuisine; to which I would add "masterful." That simple smoked mussel that so enchanted Chef Achatz was anything but simple; at least to an amateur cook like myself.

"Mussel flavor and quality changes quickly, and using just-harvested mussels is essential when smoking them," Blaine says, "otherwise their flavor gets too strong." Blaine smokes his mussels lightly—cold smoking them, on a perforated pan full of ice over a hotel pan. But first, he boils the bivalves in mussel stock for about thirty seconds, until they begin to open. He pulls the mussels free from their shells, trims their beards, and sets them on the sheet of ice and then transfers them to the smokehouse, where cool smoke will wash over them for up to five hours. Meanwhile, the mussel shells are scrubbed clean and then warmed in 300°F oven. Once the mussels achieve a delicate balance between sweet and smoky, Blaine removes them from the smokehouse and sets them into a sizzling skillet, where they are seared until deeply caramelized. The mussels are returned to their now-warm shells and each is delicately placed into a small cedar box, where they will bathe in a single puff of alder smoke piped from a handheld smoker. The lid is replaced, entombing the mussel (and the alder smoke), and the dish rushed out to the diners. Yes, these smoked mussels are simple in dress, sincere and intelligent in voice; but they undergo a preparation so lengthy and complex that only the most gifted and zealous of cooks could master this seemingly unassuming morsel.

This ardor for wood, fire, and smoke is the tenor in Wetzel's culinary voice, delivering stirring, dramatic highs in flavor regardless of ingredient. "It's not uncommon for every dish on the menu to be prepared in some way over fire," Blaine says. Throughout my dinner, it was clear many of the dishes had been kissed by smoke or licked by flame. From the smoked cod doughnuts to the pieces of smoked sockeye to the rockfish in a broth of grilled bones, the sweet flavor of smolder infused almost every protein in my meal, and many of the vegetables, too. Blaine will char scallions and blend them with raw scallions, so diners can taste the in credible contrast in flavor fire can impart on the same ingredient. He smokes tuna spines for an hour, then browns the bones in a skillet before boiling them with shiitakes to make a sublime stock. Smoked egg yolks are grated over venison tartare. After caraflex cabbage is quartered and poached with butter and verbena in a sous vide bath, it is charred over a hot flame, then finished with a sprinkling of sea salt. Whole, ripe pears are tossed into a roaring outdoor fire until the skins are black and fissured. The direct contact with red-hot flames concentrates the fruit's sugars and yields a sweetness that roasting or grilling alone cannot achieve. It's a primitive way of cooking that honors the indigenous traditions of the region while liberating the island's latent flavors.

It isn't just Wetzel's command of fire and smoke that leaves both chefs and diners in awe, as strong as it is. Rather, it is the realization that such command can only be gained from his deep understanding of the island's trees. Take red alder, for example, one of the principal tree species in the Pacific temperate rainforest, and the largest of the alder family in North America. Since the first people of Puget Sound learned to smoke fish, red alder has been the wood of choice. It is abundant, large, and its oily smoke is perfect for salmon. But Wetzel prefers green alder,

Chef Blaine Wetzel, with his sorcerer-like command of smoke and fire, readies the grill for fresh vegetables. *Courtesy of Charity Burggraaf*

another native, though less prevalent and diminutive. He finds green alder yields a more delicate smoke, which gives his dishes a gentle spice while focusing each ingredient's inherent flavor—be it egg yolks, mussels, or salmon. But it takes diligence and patience to master cooking with this species. "Green alder has to be used almost as soon as the tree is felled," Wetzel learned. "In addition, the bark can only be scraped off just before it goes onto the fire for the right flavors to come through in the food."

Blaine also relies on other trees and woody plants to create new dishes and enhance the flavor of familiar ones. He loves the perfume verbena branches lend to all sorts of produce, like those flame-burnt pears. Madrona bark is harvested as it peels away from the tree, roasted, then steeped in water to make a lovely digestive after a rich meal of lamb or deer. Meringue is made by beating one cup of heavy whipping cream with ten grams of granulated sugar and one cup of tender northern spruce tips. In between my courses of halibut with lovage stems and stinging nettles and goat's milk, I was served a tantalizing dish of toasted birch branches that would make Euell Gibbons proud. ("Ever eat a pine tree? Many parts are edible.")

I've come to regard Wetzel as the gastronomic Lorax of the Pacific Northwest; he speaks for the trees through his cuisine. Trees are his *fines herbes*, and dining at The Willows is a delicious lesson in local botany. And the ecosystem, too. Ecologists have a name for a living thing on which all other living things in the biome depend, such that if it were extinguished or diminished, the ecosystem could collapse: keystone species. When I think of the keystone species in the Pacific Northwest rainforest—or any forest, for that matter—I think trees. Each of those twenty courses I consumed at The Willows Inn were infused with flavor from the island's rich diversity of trees and shrubs. Trees are the keystone in Wetzel's cuisine, precisely because they are the keystone in the ecosystem of Lummi Island.

Knowing everything on my plate is hyperlocal, I start to piece together the biome of Lummi Island. The marine environment is easy to picture; it's obviously teeming with salmon, Dungeness crab, spot prawns, mussels, and geoduck, since that is what I'm being served. And because of Wetzel's liberal use of different wood, I *can* see the forest for the trees: an upper canopy of alder, cedar, spruce, and pine; a mid-canopy of birch and madrones; an understory of salmonberry, verbena; and then herbaceous perennials like nettles and Nootka roses. Wetzel cooks from the ecology of Lummi Island, and simply by eating his food, we diners become versed in that ecology, too.

◇◇◇◇◇◇◇◇◇◇◇◇◇◇◇◇◇◇

Eating at The Willows has changed my perspective on cooking and eating local. There is something pure and raw and transcendental about searing food over a bare flame. I now cook fish and meat almost exclusively on the grill, and a great deal of my vegetables, too. The intense heat concentrates and focuses flavors, while the smoke adds nuance and complexity. Cooking this way also means I don't need to reach for my spice rack as much. When I see how easily and readily Blaine uses trees to flavor dishes—and I don't mean the fruits and nuts, but the *wood* itself—I am surprised it isn't a more prevalent culinary practice throughout the United States. Sure, there's the occasional use of applewood when curing bacon. And North Carolina and Texas barbecue wouldn't be authentic without hickory and mesquite, respectively. But in each of these examples, only one species of tree is used with any prevalence, and then, only for a limited list of ingredients (almost exclusively pork and beef).

Thankfully, I can procure a variety of local fish and fruit and meat and mushrooms in my neck of the woods. But seasonings are perhaps the hardest to source locally. Knowing which trees, or rather which wood, can accent and enhance the innate flavors of proteins and vegetables ensures I can prepare entire meals that are deeply flavored, and deliciously so, while strengthening my connection to the environment. And I thank Blaine for teaching me such an empowering culinary—and life—skill.

SWEET DEATH

Lounging on the front deck of The Willows as the setting sun bathes everyone in a golden radiance, sipping a refreshingly stiff cocktail in between nibbles of the first of many small dishes to come, I glanced over at a soft, hand-tied, leather-bound wine list resting on the table. But a wine list with a twist. The first page is a welcome from Wetzel and an explanation that the kitchen strives to use only ingredients farmed, foraged, and fished from the island. That was followed by a few pages informing diners about his hyperlocal ingredients, and how they are raised and how they are procured; nothing pedantic, but succinctly informative. I flipped a page, looked over the hand-drawn caricature of a pink salmon, read the words *Reefnet Fishing* and almost choked on my wild nettle tostada.

Even the most sheltered diners have learned long ago of the oceanic destruction that can be wreaked from large-scale fisheries. These fisheries typically employ massive nets to catch massive quantities of fish; in the process, they disturb sensitive habitats like reefs and ocean floors, or else ensnare porpoises, sea turtles, sharks, and other large creatures unintended to be caught. I admit to my ignorance of the various nets used by commercial fisheries. I am aware of the incredible harm bottom trawling and gillnetting can do, and that the Monterey Bay Aquarium's Seafood Watch program implores fisheries to modify other netting practices to diminish ecological damage. Knowing this, and after my lengthy discussions with Amy Grondin and other trollers in the Washington area, I was convinced—at least when it comes to catching salmon—that "no netting," just hook-and-line—was the most benign to the ecosystem. "Any responsible, eco-minded chef should be buying fish exclusively from trollers," I thought.

But on this wine list was a page touting reefnet fishing, and for an instant (because *reef* and *net* sounds like an environmentalist's oxymoron), I thought I had been hooked by bait-and-switch hypocrites. Turns out, reefnetting is an age-old manner of fishing, practiced almost exclusively in America by the tribes of the San Juan Islands and Lummi Island. It is considered by environmentalists to be one of, if not *the* most environmentally friendly (and humane) way to fish commercially. And it may even yield the best flavor.

◇◇◇◇◇◇◇◇◇◇◇◇◇◇◇◇◇

Some years back, an article appeared in *The Atlantic* that opened epicurean eyes, if not unsettled our stomachs. At first blush, it appeared to be more ballyhoo over Spain's gastronomic treasure, Ibérico ham. But reading through, there were mentions of things like adrenaline, lactic acid, and cortisol, and how the color, consistency, and flavor of meat is linked to an animal's temperament right before death. Research conducted in Australia and New Zealand, as well as by Kansas State University and the U.N. Food and Agriculture Organization, revealed that anxiety adversely affects the texture and taste of meat. Journalist Daisy Freund wrote:

> When the animals are subjected to manhandling, fighting in the pens, and bad stunning techniques, the fright and stress causes a rapid breakdown of muscle glycogen. This lightens the color of the meat and turns it acidic and tasteless, making it difficult to sell, so it is usually discarded.

The industry term for this kind of flaccid and insipid meat is PSE: Pale, Soft, Exudative. And it is so rampant in the American meat industry that hundreds of millions of dollars are lost annually. (At the time the article was published in 2011, Kansas State University found the US pork industry was losing about $275 million each year from PSE.)

When I was conducting research for my book *Eating Appalachia*, I met Chris Hughes, a purveyor of exceptional antelope, venison, and wild boar meat in Texas. Hughes's experience echoed the findings from universities around the world: the handling of an animal—any handling—right before its death increases its stress and subsequently degrades the quality of its flesh. So, Hughes eliminates handling altogether.

Hughes's animals roam free on vast swaths of rangeland, relaxed and happily munching on their favorite forage. When it comes time for slaughter, his animals are not loaded into a truck and hauled dozens of miles to an abattoir, where they are herded into holding pens, then jostled down a lengthy chute, while the creatures witness their comrades just ahead getting a pneumatic hammer to the skull. Instead, the bucks and boars are still relaxed and still munching on their favorite forage—just another day in paradise—while Hughes is far away, hidden, training a sound-suppressed rifle with a precision scope on the animal's head. Within a fraction of a second, caught in mid-chew, the animal falls to the ground, lifeless. There is no time for lactic acid build-up, or to secrete adrenaline, cortisol, and other stress hormones. The result is meat that maintains its appetizing texture, color, and taste.

As it is with mammals, so it is with fish. By nature, any commercial fishing practice is stressful for the fish. Regardless if they are caught in a net or hooked on a line, there is flailing, flopping, and fighting to get free. When fish are pulled aboard, they are often gaffed and then bludgeoned. The chaos and stress may only last a couple of minutes, but that could be long enough to compromise the meat. But after watching a few YouTube videos, I wholeheartedly agree with the many environmentalists, fishermen, and chefs like Wetzel who believe reefnetting is the most respectful to the fish, and why it ensures superlative flavor.

At its simplest, reefnet fishing involves a shallow-laid net between a pair of boats. When the Native peoples of Puget Sound practiced reefnetting long ago, the boats were canoes and the nets were fashioned from cedar bark rope and marsh grasses to simulate underwater reefs. As schools of fish swam between the canoes, the men would quickly lift the net and trap the fish, then tip them into the hulls or into a holding area in the water.

Today, the boats are specially outfitted *gears* (as they are called in nautical speak), though they still appear quite rudimentary. The motors are powered by car batteries, and the decks look like they have been constructed largely of plywood. Each of the gears is outfitted with an observation tower (not unlike a crow's nest), a livewell, and in many cases, another well, the purpose of which I will explain in a moment.

Reefnet Fishing is practiced just five minutes down the road from the inn on picturesque Legoe Bay. We are lucky to be located here, since Lummi Island is one of the only places left in the world that employs Reefnetting – a native fishing method that is arguably the most sustainable and most respectful to the fish. Our catch is delivered straight from the reefnet gears to the kitchen.

An informative page from The Willows wine list.

The boats anchor just off the coast in relatively shallow water and lower a large net between them. Someone runs up the observation tower and awaits a school to swim by, over the submerged net. Once the school is spotted, the small crew is alerted below. Then, with urgent shouts of *GO! GO! GO!*, all hell breaks loose. The winches wail, the net is pulled taut and up, the gears begin to rock and sway under the tension, the fish flop wildly, and the fishermen scramble, ready for a flood of salmon to come spilling their way. One side of the net is hoisted higher than the other, and the entire school spills over onto the deck of the other gear, while the deckhands feverishly sort the fish—keepers slide into the livewell, all others are flipped back into the water. After just two chaotic minutes, calm is restored. The net is lowered back into the water, the crew takes a breather, and the salmon start to recover from the chaos in the livewell—swimming in the very same seawater they were plucked from just moments before.

◇◇◇◇◇◇◇◇◇◇◇◇◇◇◇◇◇◇

Reefnetting in Puget Sound is typically used to catch seasonal salmon—sockeye and pink during the summer months, coho and chum in the fall. Because the schools of fish are relatively small and require a couple of fishermen to help hoist the net over the gunwale and into the livewell, it is easy to identify species that don't belong. In the summer, for example, if a few chinook or coho are swimming with a school of pinks, these nontargeted species are spotted and quickly tossed back into the sea, almost perfectly unharmed. Seafood Watch reports that bycatch from reefnetting is generally nonexistent, and the mortality rate of nontargeted species released back into the water is just 0.45 percent, an astonishingly low rate that no other commercial fishing practice can come close to matching. Which is why Washington's Department of Fish & Wildlife favors this practice, declaring that "reef nets stand out as the original and still the best in selective fishing."

We can all celebrate reduced bycatch and a gentler way of catching fish. But chefs and gastronomes prize flavor above all else, and here again, reefnetting proves superior. In the recipe headnote for his luxuriously silky Smoked Sockeye Salmon, Wetzel says:

> The difference between a reefnet fish and a gill net or purse seine fish is obvious immediately upon cutting into it. The reefnet fish is bright, clean, and virtually

bloodless, while the flesh of the fish caught with other methods has a dark, dull color. The difference in flavor follows a similar parallel. Reefnet fish are fresh, firm, and clean, while the other fish have an unmistakable fishiness and a slight flabbiness, even when fresh, that I've come to identify with the blood they've retained.

Blood expulsion is crucial to fish flavor. This is why Amy Grondin's salmon are so firm and flavorful. Immediately after she lands a salmon, she inserts a pipette tip into the kidney vein and pumps saline through the fish's circulatory system, flushing every drop of blood. Reefnetters do something similar, except these fishermen rely on the salmon's natural pump—it's heart—for bloodletting.

When it is time to haul the day's catch from the gears to the market, the crew gathers around the livewell and drops to their knees. One hand reaches into the water, quickly and firmly grabbing a salmon immediately behind its gill plates, immobilizing it. The other hand deftly plucks the end of a gill free. The fish is then dropped into that other well I mentioned. It is in this tank you see crimson plumes pulsing into the sea. The salmon swim around calmly—lazily even—growing more relaxed by the second, with every heartbeat. As more blood is expunged, the fish grows more light-headed, until it slips into eternal unconsciousness. Any lactic acid that accumulated in the salmon's flesh during the netting and subsequent struggle has long dissipated, returning the meat to a pH level that will give it the appetizing firmness, rich color, and superb flavor that Wetzel says is indicative of reefnet caught fish.

◇◇◇◇◇◇◇◇◇◇◇◇◇◇◇◇◇◇

I've learned a lot about the Pacific Northwest through eating; about the landscape, the people, and their culture. But here, more so than any other place, I also learned how to honor a creature whom we are about to eat. Reefnetting taught me the importance of humane and ecologically responsible fishing—both for the environment and for flavor. After some reflection, it is clear now that this ethos is pervasive, shared by most every chef and food purveyor I met along my travels through this incredibly inspirational region. It is because of this inherent reverence for all things living that I was shown the most humane manner of killing a Dungeness crab; why Dan Severt at the Queen Anne Taylor Shellfish Oyster Bar refused to drive a toothpick through a live oyster for my martini; why Kate McDermott lit a candle and said a few thoughtful, respectful words to the geoduck before sacrificing him (her?) for our pie; and why Amy Grondin implores fishmongers, chefs, and diners alike to not judge a fish by of the color of its flesh.

Of course, the seafood of the Pacific Northwest tastes good. But eating it feels good, too. Because I know—however terrible someone might think ending a life for a single meal is—the animal on my plate was sacrificed with veneration seldom felt for any creature, whether we eat them or not. The citizens of the Pacific Northwest learned long ago the ethical, environmental, and financial importance of respecting their food sources. Because of these animals and the ubiquitous concern for their welfare, the food industry in the PNW flourishes, as do the region's ecosystems.

THE FUTURE OF AMERICAN FOOD

When I first heard about The Willows Inn, through food bloggers and foodie forums, the reviewers often depicted the restaurant as a farm-to-table jewel way off the beaten path worthy of any gastronomic journey. It sounded like my kind of eatery. A remote gustatory jewel? Perfect. *And* farm-to-table? Even better.

My meal at The Willows Inn that evening was everything

everybody said it would be—and so much more. But one thing nagged me throughout that three-hour dinner service; it was that "farm-to-table" label.

The Willows Inn is unlike any farm-to-table restaurant I've ever visited, probably because "farm-to-table" isn't the correct manner of describing Wetzel's menu. Yes, the food is seasonal and local and everything is fresh and a good deal of produce he serves is farmed; but Wetzel's menu isn't crafted around those farmed flavors, like the prototypical farm-to-table eatery is. Wetzel's cuisine is markedly different, an approach he himself describes as a "story about the land." And what a story it is! Simply by eating (and reading through the wine list), I learned a good deal about the ecology of Lummi Island and the intimate connections each ingredient shares with the others on my plate. No textbook could have taught me more about the landscape; at least, not as appetizingly so.

My visit to The Willows Inn changed my notion of what it means to eat locally and seasonally, and I recalled another salient point Chef Dan Barber made in *The Third Plate*. If you've been reading culinary journalism over the past couple of decades, you've learned a few of the perils of a Western diet: from the dramatic rise in obesity and type 2 diabetes among Americans (children included), to the decline in our soil, water, and air quality. We have been told that these concerns stem largely from our embrace of factory farming. A diet predicated on cheap carbs and bad fats, coupled with the liberal use of chemical fertilizers, herbicides, and pesticides is a five-star recipe for a sick population and an even sicker landscape. Big Ag, we've read, is the villain; but Farm-to-Table can save us.

But Chef Barber says this isn't enough. The future of the American meal shouldn't be a simple transition from mass pro-duced grains and feedlot meat and faraway, conventionally raised fruits and vegetables (what he calls the "first plate") to a dish with the *very same ingredients*, only farmed locally and organically (the "second plate"). Because buying from the farmers market, he contends, doesn't help the ecology the way we think it ought. Remember Barber's argument I quoted in the prologue: diversity is at the heart of great cuisine, but you can't have diversity if it is expensive. Farmers are business people, after all, and they typically grow that which sells. Chef Barber explains:

> Farm-to-table allows, even celebrates, a kind of cherry-picking of ingredients that are often ecologically demanding and expensive to grow. Farm-to-table chefs may claim to base their cooking on whatever the farmer's picked that day (and I should know, since I do it often), but whatever the farmer has picked that day is really about an expectation of what will be purchased that day. Which is really about an expected way of eating. It forces farmers into growing crops like zucchini and tomatoes (requiring lots of real estate and soil nutrients) or into raising enough lambs to sell mostly just the chops, because if they don't, the chef, or even the enlightened shopper, will simply buy from another farmer.

Barber argues diversity is expensive and cuisine "dumbed-down" when we empower only a few crops. He questions popular ideology that the best way to mend our broken food culture is simply to eat locally, seasonally, and organically—to choose food based upon where, when, and how we are growing it—without giving much thought to *what* we are growing. It doesn't matter much if corn, for example, is raised conventionally or organically, twelve miles from our table or twelve hundred; corn is gluttonous. It requires vast amounts of nitrogen, water, and space. "From the perspective of the vegetable gardener," Barber says, "corn is the biological equivalent of a McMansion."

"Farm-to-table may sound right," Barber acknowledges. "It's direct and connected—but really the farmer ends up servicing the table, not the other way around. It makes good agriculture difficult to sustain."

Instead, Barber champions a "third plate," a meal made with ingredients raised in accord with nature. Rather than assert our dietary preferences upon a landscape—raising produce that is not perfectly suited to the region, like tomatoes in Wisconsin—Barber advocates for allowing the local ecology to set the menu, as Wetzel does. Once we accept that our food should help maintain the balance of our ecosystems, not disturb them, indigenous flavors become central to our cuisine.

An American cuisine that arises from American biota also means a different kind of agriculture. Plowing prairies and draining wetlands so that we can cultivate field upon field of food that requires more heat / water / nutrients / pest management than the climate and environment can sustain starts to sound foolish. As an alternative, raising food becomes less about intensive row-crop monocultures and more about growing nature. It's a manner of food production that recognizes what is already abundant and flavorful in the landscape, one that "champions a whole class of integral, yet uncelebrated, crops," as Barber contends. Wetzel and his staff clear weeds and invasive plants—flavors that may not belong either on his menu or in the Lummi Island landscape—so that the indigenous flavors can shine. The Nootka rose petals and salmonberry shoots Wetzel highlights in his dishes, along with the stinging nettles, verbena branches, madrona bark, and wild grasses, feed us while helping Mother Nature tend Her crops in the Pacific Northwest—the way Native Americans did (and possibly the Archaic Indians, too). This gastronomic practice ensures the ecological diversity Barber says is fundamental to great cuisine. And anyone who has ever eaten at The Willows will surely agree.

Speaking again of the Archaic Indians, let me be clear. I'm not pledging allegiance to the food of the United States of America—something those early inhabitants of our land had

A tostada of wild native greens—my first taste of Blaine Wetzel's incomparable cuisine.

no choice but to do. Sure, I envy the Archaic Indians' incredibly diverse diet of unique ingredients. But I refuse to give up my beloved farmers market tomatoes, corn, and zucchini, even though they are resource ravenous. Nor will I ditch bananas, coffee, and mangoes anytime soon, even though they travel thousands of miles to get to my mouth. Embracing America's ancient flavors isn't a yearning for primitive subsistence. It's a desire to add spice to our meals by cultivating a fondness for the foods unique to our backyard. And this is exactly what Wetzel recognized when he arrived from Denmark and peeked inside Lummi Island's larder. Of course Wetzel uses farmed flavors in his menu. But these ingredients are merely the supporting cast in his critically acclaimed PNW cuisine. The stars of his menu—and the flavors any visitor to The Willows Inn remembers most—are those in which humans played little role, if any, in raising.

My meal at The Willows delivered what I sought at the beginning of the book. Wetzel's food is provocative, a feast for the body as well as the mind. His cuisine summarized the many brilliant, talented, and eco-minded chefs I met throughout my travels in the Pacific Northwest. His menu starts as a question—Why not eat from the landscape?—to which the diner indubitably answers at the conclusion of the meal, Why would we *not* eat from the landscape? It is these exact local sensibilities and the "profound and exhilarating sense of place" that so enthralled *New York Times* food writer Frank Bruni; the kind of cuisine that goads philosophical musings of what American food should be, the musings Seattle journalist Hsiao-Ching Chou wanted her meals to provoke.

But I also learned something else quite remarkable in that meal. Blaine—and the many other cooks I met in my visits to the Pacific Northwest, along with the fishermen and farmers and gatherers who supply these chefs with such amazing produce—taught me that an authentic American food culture is one that respects the totality of the region's ecosystem; humans, of course, but also the animals, plants, fungus, water, and soil. Even with an enticingly cheap and convenient global food supply dangling over their cutting boards, Pacific Northwestern chefs continue to be leaders in flavor *and* sustainability. Because they know eating directly from the region's landscape ensures a continued and expansive list of readily available ingredients; a list of flavors that inspires culinary creativity and sates the epicure's appetite for the unique.

Native flavors are delicious because Chef Nature intended for them to be there, and to be eaten and enjoyed. This is what Charles Lefevre taught me about Oregon truffles; Toga Hertzog about Dungeness crab; Amy Grondin and Chef Sundstrom about Chinook salmon; and Xinh Dwelley about geoduck. But it was Wetzel who pulled all these ingredients together, along with the grasses and the flowers and the berries and the fungus and the bark that grow wild and rampant in the region, to showcase what Pacific Northwest cuisine could be. Wetzel and his fellow champions of PNW produce taught me through their respective culinary tales that indigenous foods are the true ingredients of place—real gourmet foods!—and the basis of an authentic, distinctive, delicious cuisine.

THE WILLOWS RECIPES

I was initially hesitant to ask Chef Wetzel for his recipes for some of the dishes I ate that memorable evening. I mean, this guy runs one of the top kitchens in America. He was a *chef de partie* at Noma, for cook's sake! But my reticence was completely squelched after reading his book *Sea and Smoke*. Sure, a few of the dishes are time intensive and meticulously presented, requiring the incomparable skill and talent Wetzel possesses to get right. But most of his recipes are surprisingly accessible. That is, with one caveat: Blaine's dishes are ingredient driven. "Many of the recipes are so straightforward that without exceptional ingredients they are not worth attempting," he cautions.

Thankfully, exceptional ingredients are abundant, wherever we live, if only we know where to look. As fabulous as the salmon and house-cured venison and smoked mussels are at The Willows (and the sliced geoduck and poached crab and barely warmed spot prawns), what I found most tantalizing were the dishes Blaine prepares from things he forages on the island. Berries, wild grasses, nettles, pine shoots, madrona bark, beach rose petals—every plant on Lummi Island is scrutinized by Blaine; smelled and felt and tasted. This is what stands out on The Willows menu. Wetzel's proteins are some of the best I've savored; but where he really shines, where other top chefs in America are largely weak, is his mastery of wild plants. Blaine Wetzel is a modern-day Euell Gibbons, a comparison I know he would be honored to hear.

PICKLED WILD THINGS

(Makes a half pound of pickles)

Recipe courtesy of Chef Blaine Wetzel, The Willows Inn (From his book: Sea and Smoke*)*

I find the back of Wetzel's cookbook especially useful. He provides all sorts of tips, many quite simple, to create amazing condiments using fantastically unique flavors; the sorts of condiments that transform a plate of familiar food into something exotic and exciting. He offers how to's on fermenting green garlic, for example, or making capers out of seeds and underripe fruits, curing salmon roe, and simmering a stock using the local clams, mussels, and smelt.

But my favorite is Wetzel's recipe to make pickled wild things. I love this recipe because it is a delicious, easy introduction to the myriad flavors native to the Pacific Northwest, and it succinctly reveals Wetzel's culinary approach: hyperlocal flavors, simply prepared. "One of the most enjoyable parts of our job," Blaine says, "is foraging for sprouts, leaves, and berries. It is a perfect change of pace and scenery after a few hours in front of the stove. In the middle of the day, I usually run out for a quick walk, either down to the beach or along one of the forest trails to collect what's needed."

Whatever Blaine forages—fiddleheads, wild onion shoots, jelly mushrooms—he can turn into a snappy, tangy pickle. These preserved wild things are the perfect nibbler to enjoy with a cocktail on the deck of The Willows, gazing out onto the sea, right before sunset.

Please try it. It's a fantastic recipe for all sorts of shoots and fruits and mushrooms; not just those that grow in the Pacific Northwest. I guarantee it will get you excited about the wild provender in your own corner of the world.

INGREDIENTS

2 cups (450 grams) high-quality cider vinegar
1 cup (200 grams) granulated sugar
½ cup (25 grams) chopped fresh woodruff leaves and stems
1 tablespoon (5 grams) parsley leaves
1 fresh bay leaf
1 frond fresh dill (about 4 grams)
¼ teaspoon (1 gram) dill seeds
¾ teaspoon (3 grams) juniper seeds
½ teaspoon (1½ grams) whole black peppercorns
8 ounces (225 grams) wild leeks, fiddleheads, mushrooms, green
    strawberries, pine shoots—whatever you forage and fancy

PREPARATION

In a large saucepan, bring 2 cups (475 grams) of water, the vinegar, and the sugar to a boil, then simmer until the sugar has dissolved.

Place the woodruff, parsley, bay leaf, fresh dill, dill seeds, juniper seeds, and peppercorns in a large, nonreactive container and pour the hot brine over the top. Cover the container and refrigerate overnight.

Run the brine through a fine-mesh strainer and discard the solids. Bring about 1 gallon (4 liters) of water to a boil in a stockpot. While it heats, clean the fiddleheads (or ramps or mushrooms or whatever wild things you are using) of any brown or discolored or woody bits. Blanch in the boiling water for about 30 seconds, then drain and immediately plunge into an ice-water bath to halt the cooking. Once the wild things are cold, drain again and place them into the bottom of a large, plastic, nonreactive container.

Heat the brine to a simmer, pour it over the wild things, cover the container, and leave it in the refrigerator for about a week. The pickles are done when they've softened some, but still have a bit of snap to them.

NOOTKA ROSES AND SALMONBERRIES

(Makes 4 servings)

I don't know about you, but whenever I gaze upon flowers, I never think, "Mmmm, that sure looks tasty." Maybe there are a couple exceptions—squash blossoms come to mind, especially if they are stuffed with goat cheese and fried. And I suppose pansies, dandelions, and violets add colorful pop to my otherwise monochromatic leaf salad. But in these cases, the

Recipe courtesy of Chef Blaine Wetzel, The Willows Inn

flowers are merely a vessel or a garnish for the real food, adding fancy but little flavor.

At least, that is what I used to think of flowers before I had this dish from Wetzel. Of the twenty menu items I had tasted that night, this I felt best showcased Wetzel's culinary resourcefulness and creativity. And it was so pretty! The flavor is perfumed, thanks to the rosehip oil, and delightfully light. It is a charming little dish, meticulously composed; the kind of dish that brings a smile of surprise to every diner's face.

This recipe uses the delicately flavored salmonberries and Nootka rose petals because they are both native to the Pacific Northwest. But experiment; try using berries and edible flower petals that are special to the wilds around your home.

◇◇◇◇◇◇◇◇◇◇◇◇◇◇◇◇

Note: Three of the ingredients—simple syrup, verjus, and rosehip oil—are relatively easy to make at home. To make simple syrup, heat equal parts water and granulated sugar until the sugar dissolves, then refrigerate. Verjus is simply the juice from pressed, unripe wine grapes. And rosehip oil can be made by soaking dried rosehips in a small quantity of any neutral flavored cooking oil—grapeseed oil is an excellent choice—for a few days. However, most specialty food markets will have these ready for purchase.

INGREDIENTS

Salmonberry juice

6 ounces (170 grams) fresh salmonberries

Simple syrup
Verjus

For Serving

32 perfect salmonberries
64 Nootka Rose petals

Dried rosehip-infused oil

PREPARATION

Salmonberry juice

Blend the 6 ounces of salmonberries on high until they are liquefied. Strain the juice through a super fine, flexible sieve, (such as a Superbag) and refrigerate for an hour. Gently pour the juice into a separate container, leaving any particles that have settled at the bottom of the first container. Season the juice with simple syrup and verjus.

TO SERVE

Place four serving bowls in the freezer to chill. Arrange 8 salmonberries together in a circle at the bottom of each chilled serving bowl. Spoon in a tablespoon of salmonberry juice and arrange 16 rose petals on top of and against the berries. Drizzle with rosehip-infused oil, and serve immediately.

BUCKWHEAT CREPE AND HUCKLEBERRY COMPOTE

(Makes 12–15 crepes)

Recipe courtesy of Chef Blaine Wetzel, The Willows Inn

There is another remarkable treat for diners who choose to stay the night at The Willows Inn (which I highly recommend, especially if you have a cocktail on the deck before the dinner service and then opt for the wine pairing with your twenty-course tasting menu). Breakfast at The Willows is hearty farm-fresh fare, and quite a departure from the dinner menu, as all the ingredients are familiar. Fresh, local eggs, country bacon and other cured meats, cheeses, and a variety of fruits and vegetables from the farm are the morning mainstays.

Breakfast isn't as heralded as Wetzel's dinner service, and you won't find any of the dishes in his cookbook, but the meal can be as transformative. Bill Addison of *Eater* magazine noted:

Breakfast and lunch have become special meals in their own rights. They aren't extravagant whimsies of technique and imagination like dinner, but they are nevertheless occasions where sublime ingredients, like the ones my friends and I relished we when arrived, tell a plainspoken, eloquent narrative of eating on the island.

I found the same narrative as Addison. Chef Siiri Sampson, who heads the breakfast and lunch service at The Willows, miraculously coaxes new, extraordinary flavor from these familiar ingredients. For those who crave very local, very fresh (and very familiar) ingredients, The Willows breakfast is a must-try meal.

But there was one wild, native morsel on the menu that really excited me, as simple as it was: black huckleberry compote served alongside a delicate buckwheat crepe. It can be intimidating to learn a new pantry of unique vegetables and herbs, fruits and nuts. Sampson's breakfast taught me to start simple and introduce just one delicious indigenous victual to an otherwise familiar meal—a fresh, plump, perfectly ripe wild berry.

INGREDIENTS

Crepes

3 eggs
600 grams whole milk
35 grams melted butter
150 grams all-purpose flour

75 grams buckwheat flour
30 grams sugar
10 grams salt

Compote

1 pound fresh black
   huckleberries

½ pound granulated sugar
1 lemon, juiced

PREPARATION

Crepes

Mix the eggs, milk, and melted butter together, then mix into the dry ingredients. Reserve batter until ready to use.

To cook the crepe, lightly butter a nonstick sauté pan and ladle just enough batter into the hot pan to thinly cover the entire surface. When the crepe sets and is golden brown on the bottom, flip over and cook the top side until it is golden as well.

Compote

Incorporate all the ingredients in a mixing bowl, then place into a pot over medium high heat and cook the berries until they soften and release liquid. Serve warm or chilled—your preference—with the crepe.

Resources

WHEN YOU GO

Mount Hood and Mirror Lake.

◇◇◇◇◇◇◇◇◇◇◇◇◇◇◇◇◇◇

A gastronomic romp through the Pacific Northwest should be on every epicure's bucket list. And sightseer's, too. If you are visiting the region from the Midwest or the East Coast, I can only hope you have a connecting flight in California.

One of the most scenic flights in North America is from California to Seattle. Regardless if you leave from LAX, SFO, or SMF, the flight path takes you alongside the volcanoes in the Cascade Range, an incredible sight you have to see to fully appreciate, as the snow-capped peaks jut above the surrounding hillocks like Titans. Grab a window seat, and you will see Mount Bachelor and the Three Sisters, Mount Hood, and Mount Adams in the span of thirty minutes, while also flying directly over the calderas of Mount Saint Helens and Crater Lake (Mount Mazama). Mount Rainier is perhaps the most impressive, so large and so close to SeaTac it seems right outside the plane's window . . . close enough to ski down. On the other side of the plane, passengers are rewarded with views of a bustling metropolis against the tranquil waters of Puget Sound and all its charming islands.

Once you land, there are only two roads you need to know: Interstate 5 and US 101. It's rare that interstates provide both convenience and scenery, but this is yet another reason why the Pacific Northwest is a special landscape. I-5 bifurcates the Willamette Valley, crosses the spectacular Columbia Gorge, hugs the eastern shore of Puget sound, and continues onto Canada, connecting Eugene, Portland, Olympia, Seattle, and Bellingham which you would then veer from to get to Lummi Island. US 101 begins (or ends, depending on your perspective) at I-5 in Olympia and wends around the western shore of the Sound, connecting the capital city to Shelton. It then loops around the Olympic Peninsula along the Strait of Juan de Fuca through Port Townsend and Port Angeles, before heading down the breathtaking Pacific Coast. Of course, there are many more communities to see besides the ones I highlight in my book, but these two roads will connect you with the communities and flavors evocative of the region, while providing a feast for the eyes as well.

◇◇◇◇◇◇◇◇◇◇◇◇◇◇◇◇

The best time to sample native PNW flavors is during a food festival. Not only will the produce be in season and at its freshest, but nothing is more convivial and educational than a food party. You can only learn so much about unique ingredients by tasting and reading about them in solitude. Far more enlightening is to eat with others—strangers, chefs, foodies, kids—and to share your impressions with them.

The two food festivals I've highlighted in the book, along with the luncheon in Seattle, celebrate just one ingredient, be it Dungeness crab, Oregon truffles, or marbled Chinook salmon. But this is a fantastic opportunity to sample a variety of dishes to better understand each ingredient's uniqueness and utility.

The other foods I highlight—artesian water, geoduck, Olympia oysters, and wild Oregon berries—can all be sought out on your own, but try to taste them in the convivial atmosphere of restaurants.

Speaking of restaurants, if you can only visit one, then make it The Willows Inn on Lummi Island. Here, all those singular flavors are prepared in concert, for a single meal, and oh, how those dishes sing!

Oregon Truffles

Celebrating the most luxurious of gourmet ingredients, the Oregon Truffle Festival is a feast for the mind as well as the body. Packed with information and flavor, all washed down with some of the best PNW wines, the OTF is arguably the finest food festival in America. And it is an excellent opportunity to taste a host of native PNW flavors, not just truffles.

The Oregon Truffle Festival is held on two different weekends in two towns. Both weekends occur near the end of January. One weekend the festival is held just outside of Portland, in Oregon's wine country. This festival is more concise than the second weekend in Eugene, when the Joriad, the Grand Truffle Dinner, winery tours, Truffle Growers Forum, and Fresh Truffle Marketplace are all bound into one delicious and educational jubilee. Take your pick, but if you can only go to one, pick Eugene.

www.oregontrufflefestival.com

Geoduck and Olympia Oysters

Alas, the lights have been turned off at Xinh's Clam and Oyster House in Shelton. But Taylor Shellfish Farms is certainly worth a visit. Their small seafood counter offers fresh geoduck and Olympias, and other clams and oysters for purchase, plus a couple of hot chowders. It's also worth the trip to take a peek at the landscape that produces such delicious seafood. The folks there can point you to their oyster bars and other restaurants in the area, as well.

If nothing else, visit Taylor's website for a list of recipes. Many of these were created by Xinh Dwelley. We can't dine in her restaurant, but we can eat those delicious meals she once served. (I highly recommend her Mussels in Curry Sauce.)

www.taylorshellfishfarms.com/blog/recipes

Artesian Water

Olympia's public artesian well flows 24/7. Take a drink from the pipe, then walk over to McMenamin's Spar Café to sample water from the same aquifer but a different well. I also recommend trying one of their beers made with artesian water.

Spar Café: www.mcmenamins.com/spar-cafe

The city's website contains information about Olympia's artesian well, including a link to ongoing water quality test results.

http://olympiawa.gov/city-services/parks/parks-and-trails/artesian-well-commons.aspx

Dungeness Crab

"Celebrating Olympic Coast cuisine," the Dungeness Crab & Seafood Festival is the PNW's premiere crustacean celebration, and is held in Port Angeles, Washington, every October.

www.crabfestival.org/
If you fly into Seattle, the appropriately named Dungeness Line, operated by Olympic Bus Lines, provides two trips daily between Port Angeles and Seattle Tacoma International Airport. From their website: "Fare includes a beautiful ride on our luxury coaches, with free locally made chocolate chip cookies, free bottled water, free Wi-Fi, and a ferry ride between Edmonds and Kingston on the Washington State Ferries."

http://olympicbuslines.com/

If staying a few days in Port Angeles, consider taking the M/V *Coho* and visiting Victoria, British Columbia.

www.cohoferry.com/

Oregon Berries

The Oregon Berry Festival is no more. However, Portland is a fabulous origin for beginning any berry expedition. You'll need a car and good hiking shoes, but I recommend Tillamook State Forest for salal, thimbleberries, salmonberries, blackberries, black raspberries, and more.

http://tillamookforestcenter.org

For black huckleberries and Cascade bilberries, consider heading east of Portland to the Salmon-Huckleberry Wilderness Area. There are many hiking trails with excellent views and access to berries. Also, the Salmon River is excellent habitat for Chinook, Steelhead, and Coho.

www.fs.usda.gov/recarea/mthood/recarea/?recid=79441

You don't have to leave Portland to see wild berries, however. Forest Park, one of the largest urban forests in the United States, has an abundance of wild berries growing along its many trails, mainly thimbleberry, salal, and Oregon grape. Alas, municipal regulations prohibit the picking of any fruit in any public park, but Forest Park allows the opportunity to see and study the varied berry brambles native to Oregon in their natural habitat—always a good idea before ingesting any wild food:

www.forestparkconservancy.org/forest-park

And try Hoyt Arboretum, where red huckleberries abound.

www.hoytarboretum.org

Marbled Chinook

The Washington Troll Salmon Lunch is a delicious affair and perhaps the best opportunity to taste marbled Chinook. Not only will the fish be fresh, but it will be prepared by one of Seattle's best chefs, Johnathan Sundstrom.

The annual lunch is usually held on the second Wednesday of May, as a celebratory start to the Chinook fishing season. It is held upstairs at Lark Restaurant (on the Bitter / Raw mezzanine). This meal not only provides an opportunity to witness Chef Sundstrom's incredible talent, but to speak with food journalists, sample local wines, and meet the fishermen responsible for some of the highest-quality seafood anywhere in the country.

Lark Restaurant: https://larkseattle.com

Coastal Trollers Association (sponsors of the annual luncheon):

www.coastaltrollersassociation.com

An alternative source for marbled Chinook is mail order. Vital Choice— Wild Seafood and Organics is a mail order company located just north of Seattle and was founded by former Alaska fisherman Randy Hartnell. Randy has an eye for great fish and for business, and he is a consumer-friendly fish monger. His company's slick catalogs and intuitive web-site—which are packed with sumptuous photographs—make shopping for salmon a feast for the eyes. Best of all, Vital Choice sells sustainably harvested wild salmon of all species and varieties, and they practice reef-net fishing (check out their YouTube channel to learn more).

You can purchase 4-ounce or 6-ounce portions—with or without skin—to suit your family's particular tastes. I purchased Red, Ivory, and

Marbled Chinook from Vital Choice and was amazed by their customer service and expedient shipping. The price wasn't bad either.

www.vitalchoice.com

The Willows Inn, Lummi Island

This is a destination restaurant. It's not like a restaurant in the city where you might stumble across it and experience a fabulous meal without even realizing that you walked into a celebrated place. This place is so remote you will need a plane, an automobile, and a ferry. Not quite the trek Steve Martin and John Candy had to endure, but it might feel darn close.

But the meal is indisputably worth the journey. I don't think there is a finer place to taste place-based cuisine in America. Joe Ray, coauthor of *Sea and Smoke*, wrote of his meal:

> This was destination food, with clear flavors, strong technique, and beautiful presentation in a stunning place. . . . There was only one place in the world this meal could have come from. One place, and a handful of other diners and I were marveling at our luck.

Chef Blaine Wetzel is defining what Pacific Northwest cuisine could be. Little Lummi Island provides practically every ingredient Chef Wetzel needs to achieve his singular culinary goal: "I want anyone who eats at the restaurant to have the best meal of their lives," he says.

For me, I would say he succeeded.

www.willows-inn.com

Whatcom Chief Ferry Schedule: www.co.whatcom.wa.us/562 /Ferry-Schedule

BOOKS ON NATIVE PNW FOODS

There are many books about foraging for wild foods in the Pacific Northwest, and there are many cookbooks featuring PNW cuisine. But few of these delve into the indigenous flavors of the region. Here are three that gave me the greatest insight into those foods unique to the Pacific Northwest:

Gary Paul Nabhan, *Renewing Salmon Nation's Food Traditions* (Portland, OR: Ecotrust, 2006)

This slim volume is an introduction to cultural conservation through food, and a compendium of those foods that reinforce the PNW culture.

Part of the *Renewing America's Food Traditions (RAFT)* series, this book profiles both wild, native foods and domesticated heirloom varieties that were once ubiquitous staples in the culture and landscape of the region. An assortment of fungi and berries, root vegetables, fish and shellfish, and mammals—terrestrial as well as marine—are listed, many with accompanying photographs.

T. Abe Lloyd and Fiona Hamersley Chambers, *Wild Berries of Washington and Oregon* (Edmonton, AB: Lone Publishing, 2014)

This might be the definitive guide to the bramble fruits of Oregon and Washington. Salal, thimbleberries, salmonberries, huckleberries, and other fantastically unique berries native to the Pacific Northwest are deliciously described and sumptuously photographed. This was my guide as I hiked Oregon's Coast Ranges and Cascades in search of the sweetest fruits. There are even a few recipes. A true delight for any berry lover, whether you live in the PNW or not.

Rowan Jacobsen, *The Living Shore: Rediscovering a Lost World* (New York: Bloomsbury USA, 2009)

Rowan Jacobsen is arguably the foremost authority on American oyster flavor. His earlier book, *A Geography of Oysters*, is a fabulous introduction to dozens of oyster varieties along our nation's coasts. But *The Living Shore* is all about one special oyster.

"I'd long been fascinated by hundreds of varieties of oysters available in North America," Jacobsen writes, "[but] I fell in love with one tiny oyster in particular."

The Living Shore is an inspiring work about reviving the Olympia oyster population in the Pacific Northwest, and in the process, restoring estuarine health.

◇◇◇◇◇◇◇◇◇◇◇◇◇◇◇◇◇◇

I'd like to conclude this book with a sumptuous meal. For me, joy is the best reason to eat indigenously. I love discovering new flavors special to a unique locale. With so many delicious ingredients native to the Pacific Northwest, it's fun to imagine menus highlighting the various flavors.

Early in my research for this book, I reached out to celebrity Seattle chef Tom Douglas for advice and inspiration. I figured someone of his talent, intellect, and experience could point me to some fantastic native PNW foods. Chef Douglas is a three-time James Beard Award winner, winning for Best Pacific Northwest Chef, Best Restaurateur, and Best American Cookbook. He competed on Food Network's *Iron Chef*

America (and won). He has authored many cookbooks, owns a dozen eateries, and hosts the popular radio talk show *Seattle Kitchen*. On one of my flights to Seattle, I noticed Chef Douglas created a special menu for Alaska Airlines, an airline that strives to highlight local fare and flair. I asked Chef Douglas what he might cook if he wanted to showcase the myriad native flavors of the PNW. I wasn't confident he would indulge in my epicurean conceit, but Chef Douglas is incredibly gracious, and I was surprised how quickly he recalled so many indigenous ingredients.

Here is his mouthwatering menu, a testament to Chef Douglas's talent and creativity, and the bounty of native foods in the Pacific Northwest.

Tom Douglas's "Pacific Northwest Native Ingredients Sea Bar"

First Course
Cedar branch smoked Chinook salmon, wild Coppa fennel caramel
Hood canal oysters on the half shell, Douglas fir granita
Geoduck and kelp salad, duck egg

Main Course
Fire roasted black tail deer loin, chanterelle, morel, and lobster mushroom pan roast, sautéed fiddleheads, garlic, hazelnut oil, camas bulbs

Dessert
Double-crusted salal berry jam tart, huckleberry swirl ice cream, acorns

INDEX

Achatz, Grant, 193
Addison, Bill, 216–17
Alba truffles, 5, 17–18, 21–22, 27
alder, 194–96
algae blooms, 111–12
American cuisine, 4–6
anandamides, 25
appetizers
    Dungeness Crab and White
      Truffle Tartlets, 49–51, *49*
    Dungeness Crab Shooters,
      106, 121–24, *121*
    Marionberry, Salmon and Prawn
      Lettuce Cups, 154–55, *154*
Archaic Indians, 1–4, 10, 207–08
Ark of Taste, 162–63, 169
Arndt Anderson, Heather, 129,
    130, 131
Art of the Pie: A Practical Guide to
    Homemade Crusts, Fillings, and
    Life (McDermott), 77–78
Artesian Commons, 89–93, *90*
Attica Restaurant, 6
Australian cuisine, 6

Barber, Dan, 6–7, 9, 205–06, 207
Batdorf & Bronson's espresso bar,
    84

beer, 44, 86, 94–95, *96*
    cooking crab in, 102–03
berry salsa, 150–51
birds, 110, 133
Bitter / Raw, 172
blackberries, 132–34
    See also marionberries
blueberries, 127–28, 130–31, 142
books, 226–27
    See also *individual titles*
Brillat-Savarin, Jean Anthelme, 18
Bruni, Frank, 9, 209
Buckwheat Crepe and Huckleberry
    Compote, 216–18, *216*
Budd Inlet, *83*
Buttermilk Fried Oysters with
    Truffled Rémoulade, truffles,
    43–46, *43*
bycatch, 165, 202

California, 61–62, 85, 111, 113–14
Cascade Bilberries, 138–39, *139*, 223
    See also huckleberries
Cascade mountain range, 219–20
Chastain, Quinton, 101–03, *101*,
    103
Cheese, Truffled Pecorino, 41–43,
    41

Cheese Bar, The, 42
Chehalem blackberries, 132–33
Chou, Hsiao-Ching, 8–9, 99
clams, 54–56
  See also geoduck clams;
    shellfish
cocktails, Oyster Martinis, 67–70,
  67
Conklin, Neil, 99
Cook, Langdon, 145
Cordilleran ice sheet, 88–89
corn, 3, 206
cranberries, 137
Crater Lake, 129, 220

DeBenedetti, Christian, 43–44
Deur, Douglas, 138
diversity of foods, 2–3, 7, 10
dogs, 29, *30*, 40
domoic acid, 111–13
Douglas, Tom, 227–28
drinking water, 87
  See also water
drinks
  Marionberry Cocktail, 152–53,
    152
  marionberry whiskey, 150
  oyster martinis, 67–70, *67*
  See also beer; water; wine
drought, in California, 85
duck, Roasted with Huckleberry
  Relish, 156–58, *156*
Duna Chowder, 178–80
Dungeness crab, *97*, 98, *103*, *105*,
  113
  bisque, 115–18, *115*
  cooking in beer, 102–03
  cooking in seawater, 102
  killing, 107–10, 115
  meat, 104–05
  omelets, 124–26, *125*
  in pine nuts, *190*

quiche, 106
shooters, 106, 121–24, *121*
and truffles, 35
and White Truffle Tartlets,
  49–51, *49*
Dungeness Crab and Seafood
  Festival, 98–99, *100*, *105*, 114,
  222
Dungeness Crab and White
  Truffle Tartlets, 49–51, *49*
Dungeness Crab Bisque, 115–18,
  115
Dungeness Crab Omelets, 124–26,
  125
Dungeness Crab Quiche, 106,
  118–20, *119*
Dungeness Crab shooters, 106,
  121–24, *121*
Dwelley, Xinh, 58–60, 70–72, 74,
  209, 222

Eater magazine, 216–17
eggs
  Dungeness Crab Omelets,
    124–26, *125*
  quiche, 118–20, *119*
  scrambled, 12
El Gaucho, 74
Essential Oyster, The (Jacobsen), 64
Eugene, 19, 221

F/V *Duna*, *167*, 179
farm-to-table, 205–06
Feast Portland, 148
fishing, 198, 200
  See also bycatch; reefnet
    fishing; trawling; trolling
foie gras, Black Truffle Pasta with
  Marsala Cream and Foie Gras,
  46–48, *47*
food festivals, 106, 220–21
  See also *individual festivals*

food origins, 3–4
foragers, 135, 138–40, 144–46,
    197, 210, 211–12
Forest Park, 149, *150*, 223–24
Freeburg, Jason, 157
Freund, Daisy, 199
fritters, geoduck, 61, 73–76, *73*

Geoduck Ceviche, 58–59, 70–73,
    70
geoduck clams, 54–56, *55, 57,*
    192, 222
    ceviche, 58–59, 70–73, *70*
    chowder, *65*
    cleaning, 59–60, 72
    fritters, 61, 73–76, *73*
    pie, 76–81, *77*
    sashimi, *60*
Geoduck Deep-Dish Pie, 76–81,
    77
Geoduck Fritters with Rémoulade,
    73–76, *73*
Geography of Oysters, A (Jacobsen),
    63–64, 227
global agriculture systems, 2–3
Green Revolution, 7
Grilled Marbled Chinook and
    Summer Vegetables, 181–85,
    181
grilling, *195,* 196–97
    Grilled Marbled Chinook
        and Summer Vegetables,
        181–85, *181*
Grondin, Amy, 165, 169–70, *174,*
    203, 209
Grondin, Greg, *167,* 168
Gustave, 30–31, *32,* 33

hazelnuts, 159
Hertzog, Toga, 115–16, 209
high grading, 167–68
Hood, Wesley, 73–74

huckleberries, 5, 130, 137
    black, *127,* 128, 136, 139–40,
        139, 140, 223
    Buckwheat Crepe and
        Huckleberry Compote,
        216–18, *216*
    evergreen, 138
    red, 137–38
    Roasted Duck and Broccolini
        with, 156–58, *156*
    Wild Oregon Berries with
        Limoncello Cream,
        159–60, *159*
Hughes, Chris, 199–200

Indian cuisine, 22, 26
Interstate 5, 220
introduced ingredients, 4

Jacobsen, Rowan, 63–64, 227
Joriad, the, 26, 30–32

Kawahara, Joel, 165, 168, 170
king salmon, *161*
    See also salmon

Lagotto Romagnolo dogs, 29–30,
    30
Lamb, Audrey, 56–57
Lefevre, Charles, 19, *20,* 26–27, 209
Living Shore, The (Jacobsen), 227
Lloyd, T. Abe, 135, 141, 142, 148
locavores, Archaic Indians as, 3
Logan, James, 132
loganberries, 132
Luelling, Henderson, 130
Lummi Island, *15,* 188, 189–90,
    196, 220
    See also The Willows Inn

McDermott, Kate, 76–78
McGee, Harold, 21–22, 23, 25

Makah Tribe, 172
manganese, 93–94
marionberries, 132–34, 144–45
  cocktails, 152–53, *152*
  Marionberry, Salmon and
    Prawn Lettuce Cups,
    154–55, *154*
  whiskey, 150
  Wild Oregon Berries with
    Limoncello Cream,
    159–60, *159*
  See also blackberries
Marionberry Cocktail, 152–53, *152*
Marionberry, Salmon and Prawn
  Lettuce Cups, 154–55, *154*
Maxfield, Meliss, 93–94
Mirror Lake, *219*
Morgan, Ryan, 154
Morse, John, 15
Mount Hood, *219*
Mount Mazama, 129
Mount Rainier, *13*
Mount Saint Helens, 220
mushrooms, 12, 146–47
mussels, smoked, 193

New World Truffieres, 19–20
Newman, John, 46–48
Nootka Roses and Salmonberries,
  213–15, *214*

olallieberries, 132–33
Olympia, 84–85, 89–93
Olympia oysters, 5, 61–66, *65*,
  222, 227
  Martinis, 67–70, *67*
Omnivore's Dilemma, The (Pollan),
  62
Oregon Berry Festival, 128–29,
  131–32, 147, 148, 151
Oregon black truffles, *17*, 25, 35,
  36, *36*, 37

Black Truffle Pasta with
  Marsala Cream and Foie
  Gras, 46–48, *47*
Truffled Pecorino Cheese,
  41–43, *41*
Oregon Grape, 136
Oregon Truffle Festival (OTF),
  18–19, *23*, 26–27, 38–39, 40,
  49, 221
Oregon truffles, 5, *17*, 18, 21, 31,
  33–35
  See also truffles; *individual
    truffle varieties*
Oregon white truffles, *17*, 21–22,
  23, 34–35, 37
  Buttermilk Fried Oysters
    with Truffled Rémoulade,
    43–46, *43*
  Dungeness Crab and White
    Truffle Tartlets, 49–51, *49*
Oyster Martinis, 67–70, *67*
oysters, 5, *53*, 61–62
  Buttermilk Fried with Truffled
    Rémoulade, 43–46, *43*
  See also Olympia Oysters

Pacific Northwest
  delimiting, 15–16
  impressions of, 11–12, 14–16
Pacific Northwest Foraging (Deur),
  138
Pan Roasted Marbled Chinook
  with Sugar Snap Peas, Radish,
  and Morels, 175–78, *175*
Pang, Kevin, 191
pasta, Black Truffle Pasta with
  Marsala Cream and Foie Gras,
  46–48, *47*
pastry, 50–51, 78–80, 119–20
pawpaws, 4, 147–48
Pence, Caprial, 12
Périgord truffles, 5, 17, 19

persimmons, 5, 24
phytoplankton, 112
pigs, 27–28
Pollan, Michael, 62
Port Angeles, 97–98, *100*, 114, 220
Port Townsend, 165, 220
Portland, 12, 128–29, 148–50, *150*, 221, 223
prawns, Marionberry, Salmon and Prawn Lettuce Cups, 154–55, *154*
PSE (Pale, Soft, Exudative), 198–99
Puget Sound, *53*, 63, *83*, 220

quiche, Dungeness Crab, 106, 118–20, *119*

rakes, 28
raspberries, 144
Ray, Joe, 225
razor clams, 112–13
reefnet fishing, 198, 200–204, *201*
rémoulades, 44–45, 74–75
Roasted Duck and Broccolini with Huckleberry Relish, 156–58, *156*
Rothaus, Don, 112
Ruff, Charles, 35–38, 40

Sailor, Craig, 145
salal berries, 5, 8, 130, 136, 140–41, *142*
Salatin, Joel, 62
salmon, 14, 166, 170
    Atlantic, 5
    Chinook, *161*, 162–63, *164*, 167–68, *167*, *171*, 178
    Duna Chowder, 178–80
    Grilled Marbled Chinook and Summer Vegetables, 181–85, *181*
    marbled Chinook, 163–64, *164*, 167–71, *171*, 178, 224–25
    Marionberry, Salmon and Prawn Lettuce Cups, 154–55, *154*
    Pan Roasted Marbled Chinook with Sugar Snap Peas, Radish, and Morels, 175–78, *175*
    and scrambled eggs, 12
    and truffles, 37
    Wild Pacific, 5
salmonberries, 130, 142–44, *143*
    Nootka Roses and Salmonberries, 213–15, *214*
    Wild Oregon Berries with Limoncello Cream, 159–60, *159*
Sampson, Siiri, 217
Sanford, Jim, 29–30
sashimi, geoduck, 60, *60*
Schedeen, Julie, 133–34, 134
Scott, Leslie, 20, 35, 37–38
scrambled eggs, and salmon, 12
Sea and Smoke (Wetzel & Ray), 190, 193, 210, 211, 225
sea water, cooking crab, 102
Seattle, 11–12, 161–62
Severt, Dan, 68
shellfish, 14–15, 35
    See also geoduck clams; oysters
Shelton, 59, 222
Shewry, Ben, 6, 9
Slonecker, Andrea, 43–44
Slow Food, 162
soup
    Duna Chowder, 178–80
    Dungeness Crab Bisque, 115–18, *115*
Spar Café, 94–95, *96*, 222
Strait of Juan de Fuca, 113

Stump (Kevin), 68–69
Sundstrom, Johnathan, 172, 173, 174, 176, 209, 224

Tacoma, *13*
Taylor, Bill, 63
Taylor Shellfish Farms, 56–58, 62–63, *65*, 221
Thai cooking, 58–60, 71
thimbleberries, 135, 141, 144–48, *146*
    Wild Oregon Berries with Limoncello Cream, 159–60, *159*
"third plate," 207
Third Plate, The (Barber), 7
Tillamook State Forest, 149
Tippman, Marcy, 26, 30–33, *32*
tomatoes, 7–8
trawling, 165
trees/woods, as flavor, 194–97
trolling, 165–66
truffle oil, 31, 39, 40
Truffled Pecorino Cheese, 41–43, *41*
truffled salume, *39*
truffles, 21–25, *23*, 27, 34
    Buttermilk Fried Oysters with Truffled Rémoulade, 43–46, *43*
    gathering, 27-29, 33
    Oregon, 5, *17*, 18, 21, 33–35
    Truffled Pecorino Cheese, 41–43, *41*
    See also *individual varieties*
Tuber melanosporum, 19
    See also truffles

Vaccinium. See huckleberries
Velasquez, Don, 112

Vital Choice - Wild Seafood and Organics, 224–25

Waldo, George, 132–33
Wall, Michael, 118
walnuts, 4
Washington Chinook Troll Salmon luncheon, 168–69, 172, 173, *174*, 224
water, 89
    as a food, 84
    aquifers, 87–88, 94
    artesian springs, 87–88, 222
    mineral water, 85–86
    seawater, 102
    springs, 87
Wetzel, Blaine, 188–94, *195*, 202–03, 208–09, 225
Wild Berries of Washington and Oregon (Lloyd & Chambers), 135, 226
wild greens
    Nootka Roses and Salmonberries, 213–15, *214*
    pickled, 211–13, *211*
wild greens tostada, *208*
Wild Oregon Berries with Limoncello Cream, 159–60, *159*
Wild Pacific Salmon, 5
Willamette Valley, 18, 21, 27, 220
Willows Inn, 189, 190–91, *190*, 193–94, 204–05, 216, 221, 225
    See also Lummi Island
wine, 34–35, 44, 104–05
The World's Best 50 Restaurants, 6

Zenk, Karl, 49–51